# THE WI BOOK OF BISCUITS

EBURY
PRESS

# ACKNOWLEDGEMENTS

Illustrated by Ann Rees

Edited by Sue Jacquemier and Rosemary Wadey

Designed by Clare Clements

The publishers would also like to thank Cumbria-Westmorland and Cumbria-Cumberland Federations of Women's Institutes for supplying recipes for this book, and Sally Lister and Pat Hesketh for their advice and contributions.

ISBN 0 85223 302 7

Published by Ebury Press
National Magazine House
72 Broadwick Street
London W1V 2BP

First impression 1984



Filmset by
D. P. Media Limited, Hitchin, Hertfordshire

Reproduced, printed and bound in Great Britain by
Hazell Watson & Viney Limited,
Member of the BPCC Group,
Aylesbury, Bucks

# CONTENTS

# INTRODUCTION

Bake a batch of biscuits and just watch them disappear. Homemade biscuits and cookies have a special aroma and taste all of their own which is fit to tempt many a palate.

Biscuits are simple to prepare and make, and work out very much cheaper than their bought equivalents. Oats, chocolate, nuts, and many other ingredients are used to create familiar biscuits and lots of new flavours are to be found in this book. It includes many traditional types, a selection of foreign tastes and a lot of everyday biscuits which can be prepared in a matter of minutes.

Use fresh ingredients, not the leftovers from the back of the cupboard, which may be stale and would not enhance the flavour or allow the biscuits to keep in good condition for any length of time. Butter will give a better flavour than other fat but it is not strictly necessary. Biscuits should keep well for 2–3 weeks in an airtight container but it must be really airtight and the lid replaced securely each time it is opened. Once baked, biscuits should be cooled rapidly and not left around for too long before storing.

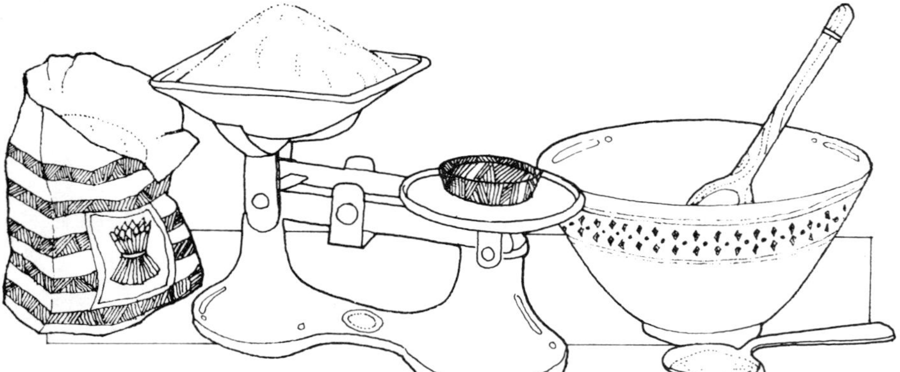

**Measurements**

All the spoon measures in this book are level unless stated otherwise.

3 tsp = 1 tbsp
8 tbsp = 5 fl oz = 150 ml = ¼ pint

Eggs are size 2 unless stated otherwise.

When following these recipes please use either the metric measurements or the imperial: do not mix them and all will be well.

Measurements for can sizes are approximate.

**American equivalents**

| | Metric | Imperial | American |
|---|---|---|---|
| Butter, margarine | 225 g | 8 oz | 1 cup |
| Shredded suet | 100 g | 4 oz | 1 cup |
| Flour | 100 g | 4 oz | 1 cup |
| Currants | 150 g | 5 oz | 1 cup |
| Sugar | 200 g | 7 oz | 1 cup |
| Syrup | 335 g | 11½ oz | 1 cup |

An American pint is 16 fl oz compared with the imperial pint of 20 fl oz. A standard American cup measure is considered to hold 8 fl oz.

# ALL SORTS OF BISCUITS

Biscuits can be eaten at any time of the day. Some are plain, some fancy, some full of fruit, others topped with icing. The selection here shows the versatility of the biscuit, with lots of old friends and a good selection of new ones too.

# COCONUT KISSES

Makes about 24

*100 g (4 oz) plain flour*
*pinch of salt*
*½ tsp baking powder*
*50 g (2 oz) caster sugar*
*50 g (2 oz) margarine*
*1 egg yolk*
*a little milk*

Topping
*1 egg white*
*50 g (2 oz) caster sugar*
*100 g (4 oz) desiccated coconut*
*glacé cherries (optional)*

Heat the oven to 180°C (350°F) mark 4. For the biscuits: sift the flour, salt and baking powder together. Mix in the sugar and then rub in the fat until the mixture resembles fine breadcrumbs. Add the beaten egg yolk and a little milk if necessary, to form a dough. Roll out the dough on a floured board and cut out shapes with a 4-cm (1½-inch) cutter. Place on greased baking sheets.

For the topping: whisk the egg white until it is stiff. Add the sugar and whisk again. Fold in the coconut. Spread the mixture on to each biscuit and top with a quarter of a cherry if liked. Bake for 25–30 minutes until the biscuits are evenly browned. Cool on a wire rack.

# ALPHABET BISCUITS

*225 g (8 oz) plain flour*
*pinch of salt*
*¼ tsp ground cinnamon*
*150 g (5 oz) butter*
*50 g (2 oz) caster sugar*
*1 tbsp water*
*caster sugar to glaze*

Icing
*100 g (4 oz) icing sugar*
*1 tbsp water*
*food colouring (optional)*

Heat the oven to 180°C (350°F) mark 4. For the biscuits: sift the flour, salt and cinnamon into a bowl, and rub in the butter until the mixture resembles fine breadcrumbs. Stir in the sugar, add the water and mix to a pliable dough. Knead until smooth.

Roll out thinly on a floured board, cut into small squares and place on lightly greased baking sheets. Brush with water and sprinkle with caster sugar to glaze. Bake for 15–20 minutes and cool on a wire rack.

For the icing: mix the sifted icing sugar with the water and beat to a smooth consistency; if liked, add a drop or two of liquid food colouring. Pipe letters on to each biscuit and leave to set.

# GIPSY CRISPS

*75 g (3 oz) cornflakes*
*225 g (8 oz) self-raising flour*
*100 g (4 oz) sugar*
*150 g (5 oz) margarine*
*2 tbsp golden syrup*
*1 tsp bicarbonate of soda*
*2 tsp boiling water*

Heat the oven to 150°C (300°F) mark 2. Crush the cornflakes and mix them with the sifted flour and the sugar. Melt the margarine and syrup and add to the dry mixture. Finally, dissolve the bicarbonate of soda in boiling water and add to the mixture. Knead together to form a dough.

Roll the dough into small round balls and place on greased baking sheets. Bake for 20–25 minutes. Cool on a wire rack.

# GROUND RICE COOKIES

*100 g (4 oz) self-raising flour*
*100 g (4 oz) ground rice*
*100 g (4 oz) caster sugar*
*100 g (4 oz) margarine*
*1 egg, beaten*
*sugar for coating*

Heat the oven to 180°C (350°F) mark 4. Sift the flour into a bowl and mix in the ground rice and sugar. Rub the margarine into the dry ingredients until the mixture resembles fine breadcrumbs then work into a dough with the beaten egg. Roll the dough into small balls and dip in the sugar.

Place on greased baking sheets and flatten slightly with a fork. Bake for 15–20 minutes. Cool on a wire rack.

# ORANGE COCONUT CRISPS

Makes about 15

*75 g (3 oz) butter or margarine*
*50 g (2 oz) caster sugar*
*grated rind of 1 orange*
*50 g (2 oz) plain flour*
*25 g (1 oz) cornflour*
*pinch of salt*
*orange juice*
*desiccated coconut*

Heat the oven to 180°C (350°F) mark 4. Cream the fat and sugar until light and fluffy, then beat in the grated orange rind. Add the sifted flour, cornflour and salt and mix to form a dough.

Shape the dough into about 15 small balls. Brush each one with orange juice and roll in the coconut. Place on greased baking sheets and flatten slightly. Bake for 18 minutes. Cool on a wire rack.

# NAPOLEON BISCUITS

*100 g (4 oz) plain flour*
*25 g (1 oz) cornflour*
*65 g (2½ oz) margarine*
*40 g (1½ oz) caster sugar*
*1 egg yolk*
*jam, any flavour*
*icing sugar*

Heat the oven to 200°C (400°F) mark 6. Sift the flour and cornflour into a bowl and rub in the fat until the mixture resembles fine breadcrumbs. Add the sugar and bind the mixture to a soft dough with the egg yolk.

Roll the dough out on a floured board to a thickness of 5 mm (¼ inch). Cut out rounds and remove their middles to make rings. Cut out an equal number of rounds the same size as the rings. Place on greased baking sheets and prick the rounds only. Bake for 10–15 minutes and cool on a wire rack.

When they are cold, spread the rounds with jam. Dust the rings with icing sugar and place on top of the jam.

# CARAWAY BISCUITS

*100 g (4 oz) margarine*
*50 g (2 oz) icing sugar, sifted*
*175 g (6 oz) self-raising flour, sifted*
*1 tsp caraway seeds*
*a little milk*

Heat the oven to 180°C (350°F) mark 4. Cream the margarine and icing sugar together until light and creamy, then add the flour and caraway seeds. Mix to form a stiff dough adding a little milk if necessary. Roll the dough out on a floured board to 5 mm (¼ inch) thick and cut into shapes. Place on lightly greased baking sheets and bake for 15 minutes or until golden brown. Cool on a wire rack.

# CHERRY WHIRLS

Makes 16–18

*175 g (6 oz) butter*
*50 g (2 oz) icing sugar, sifted*
*1 tsp vanilla essence*
*175 g (6 oz) plain flour, sifted*
*8–9 glacé cherries*

Heat the oven to 160°C (325°F) mark 3. Cream the butter until it is light and soft. Add the icing sugar and vanilla essence and beat until smooth, then stir in the flour.

Transfer the mixture to a large piping bag fitted with a large star nozzle. Pipe 16–18 fairly small whirls on to two greased baking sheets and top each one with half a cherry. Bake in the centre of the oven for 20 minutes, or until a pale gold.

Leave on the baking sheets for 5 minutes before transferring carefully to a wire rack. Store in an airtight container when cold.

# COCONUT BISCUITS

*50 g (2 oz) butter*
*75 g (3 oz) caster sugar*
*1 egg*
*75 g (3 oz) plain flour*
*25 g (1 oz) desiccated coconut*

Heat the oven to 160°C (325°F) mark 3. Cream the butter and sugar together until light and fluffy, beat in the egg then fold into the mixture followed by the flour and the coconut. Put teaspoons of the mixture on greased baking sheets and bake for 10–15 minutes. Cool on a wire rack.

# NOVELTY BISCUITS

*50 g (2 oz) margarine*
*50 g (2 oz) caster sugar*
*100 g (4 oz) self-raising flour*
*pinch of salt*
*15 g (½ oz) shelled walnuts, chopped*
*2 tsp desiccated coconut*
*15 g (1 oz) glacé cherries, chopped*
*4 tsp beaten egg*

Heat the oven to 180°C (350°F) mark 4. Cream the margarine and sugar until light and fluffy. Sift the flour and salt and mix with the nuts and coconut. Gradually add, together with the cherries, to the creamed mixture. Bind the dough together with the egg. Roll it out on a floured board and cut into shapes.

Place on greased baking sheets and bake for 15–20 minutes. Cool on a wire rack.

# HIGHLANDERS

Makes about 20

*100 g (4 oz) butter*
*50 g (2 oz) icing sugar*
*75 g (3 oz) self-raising flour*
*75 g (3 oz) plain flour*
*25 g (1 oz) demerara sugar*

Heat the oven to 180°C (350°F) mark 4. Cream the butter and sifted icing sugar until they are very light. Sift the flours together and work in to make a dough; knead thoroughly. Form the mixture into a sausage and roll in the demerara sugar. Wrap in cling film or foil, place on something flat and put in the refrigerator for at least 1 hour.

Cut into 5-mm (¼-inch) slices, and place the biscuits on ungreased baking sheets. Bake for about 10 minutes. Be careful that the edges do not burn. Remove to a wire rack and leave to cool.

# ICED GINGER SHORTCAKE

*150 g (5 oz) plain flour*
*1 tsp baking powder*
*1 tsp ground ginger*
*100 g (4 oz) butter or margarine*
*50 g (2 oz) caster sugar*

Icing
*100 g (4 oz) caster sugar*
*50 g (2 oz) butter or margarine*
*1 tbsp golden syrup*
*1 tsp ground ginger.*

Heat the oven to 160°C (325°F) mark 3. Sift the flour, baking powder and ginger together in a bowl. Cream the butter and sugar until light and fluffy. Mix the dry ingredients into the creamed mixture to make a dough.

Spread the mixture in a well greased 20-cm (8-inch) square tin and cook for 45 minutes until golden brown.

Meanwhile, prepare the icing by heating all ingredients together over a low heat. Pour over the shortcake while it is still hot. Cut it into fingers before it cools. Leave in the tin until cold.

# COFFEE KISSES

*225 g (8 oz) self-raising flour*
*75 g (3 oz) margarine*
*75 g (3 oz) caster sugar*
*1 egg*
*½ tsp coffee essence or about 2 tsp instant coffee powder*

Filling
*50 g (2 oz) butter*
*100 g (4 oz) icing sugar*
*1 tsp coffee essence or 1 tsp instant coffee powder dissolved in 1 tsp hot water*

Heat the oven to 180°C (350°F) mark 4. For the biscuits: sift the flour into a bowl then rub in the margarine until the mixture resembles fine breadcrumbs; add the sugar. Mix in the beaten egg and coffee flavouring to make a dough. Roll the dough into small balls and place on greased baking sheets. Bake for 15–20 minutes and cool on a wire rack.

To make the filling: cream the butter until it is soft then gradually beat in the sifted icing sugar. Add the coffee flavouring and beat well.

When the biscuits are cold, sandwich together with the filling.

# LEMON CRESCENTS

*grated rind and juice of ½ lemon*
*50 g (2 oz) caster sugar*
*50 g (2 oz) butter*
*100 g (4 oz) plain flour*
*1 egg, beaten*
*chopped almonds*

Heat the oven to 180°C (350°F) mark 4. Rub the grated lemon rind and the sugar in a basin until the sugar is yellow. Rub the butter into the sifted flour until it resembles fine breadcrumbs. Add the lemon juice and sugar and sufficient egg to bind together.

Roll the dough out thinly on a floured board and cut into crescent shapes. Place on a greased baking sheet. Brush with the remaining beaten egg and sprinkle with chopped almonds. Bake for 20 minutes. Cool on a wire rack.

# EASTER BUNNY BISCUITS

*75 g (3 oz) soft margarine*
*100 g (4 oz) caster sugar*
*1 egg*
*225 g (8 oz) plain flour*
*pinch of salt*
*2 tsp mixed spice*
*25 g (1 oz) currants*

Coating
*egg white*
*desiccated coconut*

*extra currants to decorate*

Heat the oven to 190°C (375°F) mark 5. Cream the fat and sugar until light and fluffy. Beat in the egg thoroughly, then fold in the sifted flour, salt, and spice. Add the currants and mix well to form a dough.

Roll the dough out on a floured board to a thickness of 5 mm (¼ inch). Cut out the biscuits with a rabbit-shaped cutter. Brush with egg white and dip in the coconut. Add a currant to each one to represent an eye.

Place the biscuits on greased and floured baking sheets and bake the biscuits near the top of the oven for 15–18 minutes. Remove carefully to a wire rack and leave to cool.

# GINGER RUFFLES

*100 g (4 oz) self-raising flour*
*½ tsp bicarbonate of soda*
*1 tsp ground ginger*
*50 g (2 oz) margarine*
*50 g (2 oz) caster sugar*
*2 tbsp golden syrup*

Heat oven to 180°C (350°F) mark 4. Sift the flour, soda and ginger into a bowl. Rub in the margarine until the mixture resembles fine breadcrumbs, then add the sugar. Warm the syrup, add to the mixture and work well together.

Divide the dough into two pieces and form each one into a long sausage. Place each one in the middle of a greased baking sheet. Bake at the top of the oven for about 20 minutes. Remove from the oven and cut into strips while still warm. Cool the biscuits on a wire rack.

## GINGER SNAPS

*100 g (4 oz) margarine*
*4 tbsp golden syrup*
*225 g (8 oz) plain flour*
*pinch of salt*
*1 tsp ground ginger*
*100 g (4 oz) caster sugar*
*1 egg yolk*
*½ tsp bicarbonate of soda*
*a little milk*
*caster sugar*

Heat the oven to 190°C (375°F) mark 5. Melt the margarine and the syrup together in a pan. Sift the flour, salt and ginger into a bowl and stir in the sugar. Blend in the melted margarine and syrup and the beaten egg yolk. Dissolve the soda in a little warm milk and add to the mixture.

Turn the dough on to a floured board and knead until smooth. Roll out thinly on a sugared board and cut into rounds about 6 cm (2½ inches) in diameter. Place on greased and floured baking sheets and bake for 15–20 minutes. Allow to set on the baking sheet then remove to a wire rack and leave to cool.

## ORANGE CREAMS

Makes about 12 pairs

*100 g (4 oz) margarine*
*100 g (4 oz) caster sugar*
*2 tsp golden syrup*
*finely grated rind of 1 small orange*
*1 egg yolk*
*150 g (6 oz) plain flour*
*25 g (1 oz) custard powder*
*½ tsp cream of tartar*
*½ tsp bicarbonate of soda*

Filling
*40 g (1½ oz) butter*
*75 g (3 oz) icing sugar, sifted*
*a little grated orange rind*
*about 1 tsp orange juice*

Grease two or three baking sheets. Heat the oven to 190°C (375°F) mark 5. Cream the margarine and sugar together until very light and fluffy. Beat in the syrup, orange rind and egg yolk. Sift the flour, custard powder, cream of tartar and soda together and work into the creamed mixture.

Roll the mixture into balls the size of a small walnut and put on to the baking sheets allowing room for spreading. Bake for about 20 minutes or until golden brown. Remove carefully to a wire rack and leave to cool.

For the filling: cream the butter and sugar together, then beat in the orange rind and sufficient orange juice to give a thick spreading consistency. Use the orange butter cream to sandwich the biscuits together when they are cool.

# PEANUT BUTTER COOKIES

*1 tbsp peanut butter*
*grated rind of ½ orange*
*50 g (2 oz) butter*
*50 g (2 oz) caster sugar*
*3 tbsp soft light brown sugar*
*1 egg, beaten*
*100 g (4 oz) self-raising flour*

Heat the oven to 180°C (350°F) mark 4. Cream the peanut butter, orange rind, butter and both sugars until the mixture is light and fluffy. Work in the beaten egg and stir in the sifted flour to make a firm dough.

Roll the dough into walnut-sized pieces and place, spaced well apart, on greased baking sheets. Dip a fork in a little flour and press criss-cross lines on top of each one. Bake for 25 minutes until risen and golden brown. Cool on a wire rack.

# RICE BISCUITS

*225 g (8 oz) self-raising flour, sifted*
*100 g (4 oz) ground rice*
*175 g (6 oz) caster sugar*
*175 g (6 oz) margarine*
*4 tbsp milk*
*¼ tsp lemon essence*
*glacé cherries*

Heat the oven to 180°C (350°F) mark 4. Mix the flour, rice and sugar together in a bowl. Rub in the margarine until the mixture resembles fine breadcrumbs. Mix to a stiff dough with the milk and lemon essence.

Roll the dough out thinly on a floured board and cut into rounds with a plain or fluted cutter 6 cm (2½ inches) in diameter. Decorate each one with a small piece of cherry. Place on greased baking sheets and bake for about 15 minutes, then cool on a wire rack.

# COCONUT CRISPS

*225 g (8 oz) self-raising flour, sifted*
*225 g (8 oz) soft margarine*
*75 g (3 oz) icing sugar*
*drop of vanilla essence*
*25 g (1 oz) desiccated coconut*

Heat the oven to 160°C (325°F) mark 3. Cream all the ingredients together except the coconut. Form the mixture into small balls and roll in the coconut. Place on greased baking sheets and bake for about 20 minutes or until they are golden brown. Cool on a wire rack.

# RICH BISCUITS

Makes about 40

*225 g (8 oz) self-raising flour*
*100 g (4 oz) caster sugar*
*100 g (4 oz) margarine or butter*
*grated rind and juice of ½ lemon*
*1 egg, beaten*

Heat the oven to 180°C (350°F) mark 4. Sift the flour into a bowl and mix in the sugar. Rub in the margarine until the mixture resembles fine breadcrumbs. Add the grated lemon rind and mix to a stiff dough with the beaten egg and lemon juice.

Roll the dough out thinly on a floured board and cut into approximately 40 rounds with a scone cutter about 5 cm (2 inches) in diameter. Bake for about 15 minutes. Cool on a wire rack.

# SWEETMEAL COOKIES

Makes 16–18

*75 g (3 oz) wholemeal flour*
*15 g (½ oz) plain flour*
*pinch of salt*
*½ tsp baking powder*
*15 g (½ oz) fine oatmeal*
*40 g (1½ oz) butter or margarine*
*40 g (1½ oz) caster sugar*
*about 2 tbsp milk*

Grease two baking sheets. Heat the oven to 190°C (375°F) mark 5. Mix the wholemeal flour with the sifted plain flour, salt and baking powder in a bowl and add the oatmeal. Add the butter and rub in until the mixture resembles fine breadcrumbs. Stir in the sugar and add sufficient milk to mix to a stiff paste. Knead well.

Roll out thinly on a lightly floured surface and cut into rounds using a plain or fluted 5 or 6-cm (2 or 2½-inch) cutter. Transfer to the baking sheets and prick well all over. Bake for 15–20 minutes or until a light golden brown. Cool on a wire rack and store in an airtight container.

*Variation*
If made small they may be sandwiched together with a flavoured butter cream.

# FRUITY SNAPS

*50 g (2 oz) sultanas*
*25 g (1 oz) caster sugar*
*50 g (2 oz) margarine*
*4 tbsp golden syrup*
*150 g (5 oz) self-raising flour, sifted*

Heat the oven to 180°C (350°F) mark 4. Place the sultanas, sugar, margarine and syrup in a pan and warm over a low heat until the fat melts. Take care that the mixture does not overheat. Remove from the heat, add the flour and beat well.

Place small tablespoons of the mixture well apart on greased baking sheets. Bake for about 12–15 minutes until golden brown. Allow to set before removing from the baking sheets, but do not leave for too long or they will stick. Cool on a wire rack.

# COFFEE COOKIES

Makes 20–25

*75 g (3 oz) butter*
*50 g (1½ oz) caster sugar*
*½ tsp almond essence*
*100 g (4 oz) self-raising flour, sifted*
*1 tsp instant coffee powder*
*2 tsp water*

Icing
*½ tsp instant coffee powder*
*2 tsp warm water*
*3 tbsp icing sugar sifted*
*a few decorations (optional)*

Grease two baking sheets. Heat the oven to 180°C (350°F) mark 4. Cream the butter, sugar and essence together until very light and fluffy, then gradually work in the flour. Dissolve the coffee in the water and add to the mixture to form a pliable dough.

Divide the mixture into 20–25 equal pieces and roll into balls. Place on the baking sheets and flatten with a fork. Alternatively roll out the dough thinly on a lightly floured board and cut into shapes using a variety of biscuit cutters; place on the baking sheets.

Bake in the centre of the oven for 15–20 minutes until just firm. Remove carefully with a palette knife and cool on a wire rack.

For the icing: dissolve the coffee powder in the water and gradually beat in the icing sugar until smooth. Put a small amount on to each biscuit and if liked top with a piece of walnut, crystallized violet or rose petal, etc., and leave to set.

# APRICOT SHORTCAKES

*175 g (6 oz) plain flour*
*100 g (4 oz) butter*
*50 g (2 oz) ground rice*
*50 g (2 oz) caster sugar*
*40 g (1½ oz) apricot jam*
*extra jam for decoration*
*extra caster sugar*

Heat the oven to 180–190°C (350–375°F) mark 4–5. Sift the flour into a bowl and rub in the butter until the mixture resembles fine breadcrumbs. Add the ground rice and sugar and mix together. Put the jam in the centre of the mixture and work into a smooth dough.

Roll out on a floured board to about 2 cm (¾ inch) thick. Cut into fancy shapes. Place on greased baking sheets. Make a small hollow in the centre of each biscuit with a thimble and put a little jam in the hole. Bake for about 20 minutes. Cool on a wire rack and when the biscuits are cold, dredge with caster sugar.

# BASIC DROP COOKIES

*75 g (3 oz) margarine*
*75 g (3 oz) caster sugar*
*1 egg, beaten*
*225 g (8 oz) plain flour*
*½ tsp baking powder*
*3 tbsp milk*
*½ tsp vanilla essence*

Heat the oven to 180°C (350°F) mark 4. Cream the margarine and sugar until light and fluffy then add the beaten egg. Sift the flour and baking powder together and add to the creamed mixture alternating with the milk and vanilla essence. Not all the milk may be needed as the mixture must not be too soft.

Drop teaspoons of the mixture on to a greased baking sheet, leaving room for the biscuits to spread. Bake for 10–16 minutes, then cool on a wire rack.

*Variations*

(1) Substitute soft brown sugar for caster sugar to make a light brown cookie.
(2) Fruit and nut cookie: add 75 g (3 oz) dried fruit and 25 g (1 oz) chopped nuts.
(3) Cinnamon wafer: add 1 tsp ground cinnamon to the dry ingredients.

(4) Chocolate wafer: substitute 1 tbsp cocoa for 25 g (1 oz) flour.
All the cookies may be iced and decorated.

## CARAWAY MOMENTS

Makes 30

*75 g (3 oz) butter or margarine*
*75 g (3 oz) lard or white fat*
*125 g (5 oz) light soft brown sugar*
*1 egg, beaten*
*275 g (10 oz) self-raising flour, sifted*
*1 tsp vanilla essence*
*½ tsp caraway seeds*
*about 50 g (2 oz) cornflakes, crushed*
*8 glacé cherries, quartered*

Grease two or three baking sheets. Heat the oven to 180°C (350°F) mark 4. Beat the fats together until well blended, add the sugar and cream together until light and fluffy. Beat in the egg then gradually mix in the flour, essence and caraway seeds to give a fairly stiff dough.

Divide the mixture into 30 pieces and roll each into a ball. Roll in the crushed cornflakes and place fairly well apart on the baking sheets. Flatten each slightly and top each one with a piece of glacé cherry. Bake for 15–20 minutes or until golden brown. Cool on a wire rack and store in an airtight container.

## GINGER BISCUITS

*100 g (4 oz) margarine*
*100 g (4 oz) caster sugar*
*1 tbsp treacle*
*1 tbsp golden syrup*
*225 g (8 oz) self-raising flour*
*1 tsp ground ginger*
*1 tsp bicarbonate of soda*
*a little hot water*

Heat the oven to 180°C (350°F) mark 4. Cream the margarine and sugar until light and fluffy. Warm the treacle and syrup and add to the creamed mixture with the sifted flour and ginger. Dissolve the soda in a little hot water and stir into the mixture. Mix thoroughly.

Roll the dough into balls and place on greased baking sheets. Bake for 15 minutes. Cool on a wire rack.

# ICED RASPBERRY BISCUITS

*75 g (3 oz) margarine*
*75 g (3 oz) caster sugar*
*1 egg*
*200 g (7 oz) plain flour*
*pinch of salt*

Filling
*raspberry jam*

Icing
*100 g (4 oz) icing sugar*
*1 tbsp water*

Heat the oven to 200°C (400°F) mark 6. Cream the margarine and sugar until light and fluffy then beat in the egg. Sift the flour and salt into the mixture and knead together. Roll out the dough on a lightly floured board and cut into rounds with a medium-sized cutter. Place on greased baking sheets and bake for 8–10 minutes. Cool on a wire rack. When cold, sandwich together with the raspberry jam.

To make the icing: mix the sifted icing sugar with the water and beat to a smooth consistency. Spread the icing over the tops of the biscuits and leave to set.

# FREEZER BISCUITS

*1 egg, beaten*
*200 g (7 oz) caster sugar*
*200 g (7 oz) plain flour*
*1 tsp baking powder*
*½ tsp salt*
*100 g (4 oz) butter or soft margarine*

Mix together the egg and sugar. Sift the flour into a bowl with the baking powder and salt and add any flavouring (see variations). Melt the butter or use soft margarine and add this to the mixture to make a soft dough.

Knead lightly, then form into a sausage shape 2.5 cm (1 inch) in diameter. Wrap in greaseproof paper or cling film and place in the freezer or refrigerator until needed. Defrost if frozen until soft enough to cut. Cut off slices about 5 mm (¼ inch) thick and place on greased baking sheets. Bake for 15–20 minutes at 180°C (350°F) mark 4. Cool on a wire rack.

*Variations*
(1) 1 tsp vanilla essence and 50 g (2 oz) chopped walnuts.
(2) 1 tsp almond essence and 50 g (2 oz) chopped almonds.
(3) 1 tsp ground ginger and 50 g (2 oz)

chopped crystallized or stem ginger.
(4) 50 g (2 oz) grated chocolate and 1 tsp vanilla essence.
(5) 1 tbsp instant coffee powder and 50 g (2 oz) chopped walnuts.
(6) Grated rind of 1 lemon and 50 g (2 oz) currants.
(7) 1 tsp vanilla essence and 1 tbsp instant coffee powder.
(8) Use soft brown sugar instead of caster sugar and add 1 tsp vanilla essence and 50 g (2 oz) chopped raisins.

## RAISIN SHORTCAKE

*4 tbsp orange juice*
*100 g (4 oz) seedless raisins*
*175 g (6 oz) plain flour*
*100 g (4 oz) butter*
*50 g (2 oz) caster sugar*

Heat the oven to 180°C (350°F) mark 4. Put the orange juice and raisins into a pan and bring slowly to the boil. Leave to cool. Sift the flour into a bowl and rub in the butter until the mixture resembles fine breadcrumbs. Add the sugar and knead the dough well, then divide it into two equal portions.

Shape each piece into a round and place one on a greased baking sheet. Spread with the raisin mixture and top with the second round; press firmly together. Prick well all over and bake for 30 minutes. Mark into sections. Remove from the baking sheet when cold and break up into pieces.

# CRISPS

Makes about 36

*175 g (6 oz) margarine*
*100 g (4 oz) soft brown sugar*
*100 g (4 oz) self-raising flour*
*1 tsp baking powder*
*100 g (4 oz) bran buds*

Heat the oven to 180°C (350°F) mark 4. Cream the margarine and sugar together until light and fluffy. Sift the flour and baking powder and add to the mixture followed by the bran buds. Knead together to form a dough.

Roll the dough into small balls and place on greased baking sheets. Bake for about 15 minutes or until golden brown. Cool on a wire rack.

# BURNT BUTTER BISCUITS

*100 g (4 oz) butter*
*100 g (4 oz) caster sugar*
*1 egg, beaten*
*175 g (6 oz) self-raising flour*

Heat the oven to 180°C (350°F) mark 4. Put the butter in a saucepan and cook until it is golden brown. Pour into a bowl and leave it to cool. When the butter has just set, mix in the sugar and beat well. Add the egg and then gradually work in the sifted flour to make a stiff dough.

Roll the dough into small balls, place on greased baking sheets and bake for about 15 minutes. Cool on a wire rack.

# COCONUT RINGS

Makes 16–18

*100 g (4 oz) plain flour*
*100 g (4 oz) caster sugar*
*100 g (4 oz) butter or margarine*
*100 g (4 oz) desiccated coconut*
*1 egg, beaten*
*raspberry jam*

Lightly grease two baking sheets. Heat the oven to 190°C (375°F) mark 5. Sift the flour into a bowl and mix in the sugar. Add the fat and rub in until the mixture resembles breadcrumbs, then stir in the coconut. Bind to a fairly soft but manageable dough with the egg.

Knead the dough lightly and roll out thinly on a floured surface. Cut into rounds using a 6-cm (2½-inch) plain or fluted cutter, then stamp out the centres using a 2.5-cm (1-inch) cutter. Put the rings on a baking sheet. Re-roll the trimmings and cut out more rings.

Bake for about 15 minutes or until lightly tinged brown. Cool on a wire rack and when cold sandwich together in pairs with the raspberry jam.

# YO-YO'S

*175 g (6 oz) margarine*
*50 g (2 oz) icing sugar, sifted*
*175 g (6 oz) self-raising flour*
*50 g (2 oz) custard powder*
*½ tsp vanilla essence*

Filling
*50 g (2 oz) butter*
*100 g (4 oz) icing sugar*
*2–3 drops vanilla essence*

Heat the oven to 180°C (350°F) mark 4. For the biscuits: cream the margarine and icing sugar until light and fluffy. Work in the sifted flour and custard powder followed by the vanilla essence.

Roll the dough into balls and place on greased baking sheets. Mark with the back of a fork. Bake for 10 minutes. Cool on a wire rack.

To make the filling: cream the butter until it is soft. Gradually beat in the sifted icing sugar and the vanilla essence and beat until smooth. Sandwich the biscuits together with the filling.

## CINNAMON BARS

*100 g (4 oz) margarine*
*75 g (3 oz) caster sugar*
*½ egg*
*125 g (5 oz) plain flour*
*2 tsp ground cinnamon*
*pinch of salt*
*chopped nuts*

Heat the oven to 140°C (275°F) mark 1. Cream the margarine and sugar until they are light and fluffy. Beat in the egg, reserving a little of the white for glazing. Sift the flour, cinnamon and salt together and gradually add to the creamed mixture.

Press the dough into a greased oblong tin approximately 18 x 28 cm (7 x 11 inches). Brush the surface with egg white and sprinkle with chopped nuts. Bake for 1 hour. Cut into slices and allow to cool in the tin, then remove carefully and store in an airtight container.

## CHESTNUT BISCUITS

*100 g (4 oz) butter*
*100 g (4 oz) caster sugar*
*1 egg yolk*
*225 g (8 oz) plain flour, sifted*
*1 tsp chestnut purée, sweet or natural*

Heat the oven to 150–160°C (300–325°F) mark 2–3. Cream the butter and sugar until light and fluffy. Add the egg yolk and flour and lastly the purée. Knead together thoroughly.

Roll out the dough on a lightly floured board and cut into rounds approximately 5 cm (2 inches) in diameter. Place them on greased baking sheets and bake for 30 minutes or until they are golden brown. Cool on a wire rack.

## SEMOLINA PYRAMID BISCUITS

*75 g (3 oz) butter*
*50 g (2 oz) sugar*
*50 g (2 oz) cornflour*
*25 g (1 oz) semolina*
*a little jam, any flavour*

Heat the oven to 180°C (350°F) mark 4. Cream the butter and sugar until light and fluffy. Mix the cornflour and semolina and add to the creamed mixture to form a dough. Knead well.

Roll the dough out thinly on a floured

board. Cut out equal numbers of rounds with a 2.5-cm (1-inch) fluted cutter, a 4-cm (1½-inch) plain cutter, and a 5-cm (2-inch) fluted cutter. Put the rounds on greased baking sheets and bake for 15 minutes. Cool on a wire rack.

When the biscuits are cold, sandwich the three rounds together with jam to form a pyramid.

# KELVIN CRISPS

*100 g (4 oz) plain flour*
*½ tsp ground cinnamon*
*½ tsp baking powder*
*100 g (4 oz) butter or margarine*
*75 g (3 oz) caster sugar*
*75 g (3 oz) desiccated coconut*
*1 egg, beaten*

Heat the oven to 180°C (350°F) mark 4. Sift the flour, cinnamon and baking powder into a bowl, then rub in the fat until the mixture resembles breadcrumbs. Add the remainder of the dry ingredients and mix together with the well beaten egg to make a fairly stiff dough.

Roll the dough out on a lightly floured board to a thickness of 5 mm (¼ inch). Stamp out into small rounds and place on greased baking sheets. Bake for 15 minutes. Cool on a wire rack.

*Variations*
When they are cold, serve the biscuits:
(1) Topped with a dab of melted chocolate and half a glacé cherry.
(2) Sandwiched together with apricot jam.

# COCONUT DROPS

*2 egg whites*
*100 g (4 oz) granulated sugar*
*225 g (8 oz) desiccated coconut*

Heat the oven to 180°C (350°F) mark 4. Beat the egg whites until stiff and dry. Add the sugar and coconut and beat them all together.

Drop small teaspoons of the mixture on to baking sheets lined with greased greaseproof paper or non-stick parchment and bake for about 20 minutes. Cool on a wire rack.

# HONEY BISCUITS

*100 g (4 oz) unsalted butter*
*6 tbsp clear honey*
*50 g (2 oz) caster sugar*
*1 tsp bicarbonate of soda*
*1 egg yolk*
*100 g (4 oz) plain flour*
*100 g (4 oz) sugar lumps*

Heat the oven to 200°C (400°F) mark 6. Melt the butter and pour it into a large bowl. As it begins to cool, stir in the honey, caster sugar, soda and egg yolk. Add the sifted flour gradually and mix to form a firm dough.

Roll rounded teaspoons of the mixture into balls on a floured board. Coarsely crush the sugar lumps and dip the top of each ball into it. Place the balls on baking sheets lined with non-stick baking parchment and bake for 12 minutes. Cool on a wire rack.

# OATMEAL BISCUITS

*150 g (5 oz) plain flour*
*1 tsp baking powder*
*175 g (6 oz) coarse oatmeal*
*100 g (4 oz) caster sugar*
*75 g (3 oz) butter*
*a little milk*

Heat the oven to 150°C (300°F) mark 2. Sift the flour and baking powder into a bowl, and add the oatmeal and sugar. Rub the butter into the dry ingredients, then add the milk and mix to form a dough. Roll out the dough on a lightly floured board and cut into shapes. Place the biscuits on well greased baking sheets and bake for 15–20 minutes. Cool on a wire rack.

# WHOLEMEAL SHORTCAKE

*100 g (4 oz) butter*
*50 g (2 oz) Barbados sugar*
*225 g (8 oz) plain wholemeal flour*
*pinch of salt*
*25 g (1 oz) ground almonds*
*½ egg yolk*

Heat the oven to 160°C (325°F) mark 3. Cream the butter and sugar until they are soft and fluffy. Stir in the dry ingredients then add the egg yolk and work together to form a dough. Roll the dough out on a floured surface and cut into pieces or rounds approximately 6–7.5 cm (2½–3 inches) in diameter. Bake for about 15–20 minutes. Cool on a wire rack.

# LEMON FUDGE BISCUITS

*225 g (8 oz) plain 'tea' biscuits*
*50 g (2 oz) desiccated coconut*
*grated rind of ½ lemon*
*100 g (4 oz) butter or margarine*
*200 g (7 oz) condensed milk*

Icing
*a few drops of yellow food colouring*
*1½ tbsp lemon juice*
*175 g (6 oz) icing sugar*

For the base: crush the biscuits (the easiest way is to put the biscuits in a polythene bag and crush with a rolling pin) then add the coconut and lemon rind. Melt the butter and add the condensed milk. Add to the dry ingredients and mix thoroughly. Press the mixture into a greased Swiss roll tin.

To prepare the icing: add the yellow food colouring to the lemon juice and mix in the sifted icing sugar. Spread the icing over the base and leave to set. Cut the biscuits into shapes.

# DREAM COOKIES

*100 g (4 oz) soft margarine*
*75 g (3 oz) caster sugar*
*150 g (5 oz) plain flour*
*pinch of salt*
*½ tsp baking powder*
*1–2 drops vanilla essence*
*blanched almonds*

Heat the oven to 180°C (350°F) mark 4. Cream the margarine and sugar until light and fluffy. Sift the flour with the salt and baking powder and work into the creamed mixture with the vanilla essence.

Roll the dough into small balls, place on greased baking sheets and top each one with an almond. Bake for 15–20 minutes or until pale gold. Cool on a wire rack.

# AUNTIE DOT'S BISCUITS

Makes 18

*75 g (3 oz) butter or margarine*
*75 g (3 oz) caster sugar*
*75 g (3 oz) self-raising flour, sifted*
*a little egg*
*75 g (3 oz) raisins*
*cornflakes*

Heat the oven to 180°C (350°F) mark 4. Cream the fat and sugar until light and fluffy. Stir in the flour and about half a beaten egg or sufficient egg to make a very stiff dough, then knead in the raisins.

Roll teaspoons of the mixture into balls, then roll them in cornflakes. Place on greased baking sheets, leaving plenty of room for them to spread. Bake for about 12 minutes then cool on a wire rack.

# BUTTER COOKIES

*175 g (6 oz) butter*
*100 g (4 oz) soft brown sugar*
*225 g (8 oz) plain flour, sifted*
*25 g (1 oz) demerara sugar*

Heat the oven to 180°C (350°F) mark 4. Cream the butter and the brown sugar until light and fluffy. Work in the flour to give a smooth dough. Divide in half and form each piece into a sausage shape, then roll each in the demerara sugar. Wrap in cling film or foil and cool in the refrigerator until they are quite firm.

Cut into slices and place on greased baking sheets. Bake for 20 minutes then cool on a wire rack.

# COCONUT BUTTER BISCUITS

*175 g (6 oz) butter*
*2 tbsp golden syrup*
*100 g (4 oz) desiccated coconut*
*225 g (8 oz) self-raising flour*
*½ tsp bicarbonate of soda*
*175 g (6 oz) caster sugar*

Heat the oven to 180°C (350°F) mark 4. Melt the butter and syrup in a pan then add the coconut. Sift the flour and soda into the mixture and stir well. Lastly stir in the caster sugar.

Shape the dough into small balls, and place on greased baking sheets leaving room for the biscuits to spread. Bake for 12–15 minutes. Cool on a wire rack.

# KRINGLES

Makes about 48

*225 g (8 oz) plain flour*
*2 tsp baking powder*
*100 g (4 oz) butter*
*225 g (8 oz) caster sugar*
*1 egg*
*3 tbsp brandy*
*2 tsp caraway seeds*
*caster sugar for dredging*

Heat the oven to 190°C (375°F) mark 5. Sift 175 g (6 oz) of the flour with the baking powder. Cream the butter and sugar until soft and then beat in the egg, brandy and caraway seeds. Stir in the sifted flour, then add enough of the remaining 50 g (2 oz) of flour to make a stiff dough that you can handle. Cover and chill thoroughly.

Roll the dough out on a floured board to a thickness of 2.5 mm (1/8 inch). Cut into shapes and put on ungreased baking sheets. Sprinkle with caster sugar and bake for 15 minutes. Cool on a wire rack.

# CRUNCHY BISCUITS

*100 g (4 oz) butter or margarine*
*75 g (3 oz) caster sugar*
*1 tbsp golden syrup*
*100 g (4 oz) self-raising flour, sifted*
*100 g (4 oz) rolled oats*
*pinch of salt*
*pinch of bicarbonate of soda*

Topping
*175 g (6 oz) cooking chocolate, plain or milk*

Heat the oven to 180°C (350°F) mark 4. Cream the butter, sugar and syrup together, then mix in the dry ingredients. Roll the dough into small balls. Place on greased baking sheets and press flat with a fork. Bake for 15–20 minutes. Cool on a wire rack. When the biscuits are cold, cover with melted chocolate.

# CHRISTMAS TREE COOKIES

*150 g (6 Oz) butter*
*150 g (6 oz) caster sugar*
*1 egg, separated*
*grated rind of 1 orange*
*150 g (6 oz) plain flour*
*50 g (2 oz) self-raising flour*
*icing sugar to dust*

Grease two or three baking sheets. Heat the oven to 190°C (375°F) mark 5.

Cream the butter until soft, add the sugar and beat until light and fluffy. Reserve a little egg white for glazing and add the rest of the egg to the mixture. Beat in the orange rind and fold in the sifted flours. Knead lightly until smooth, wrap in cling film or foil and chill for 30 minutes.

Roll out the dough on a lightly floured board to about 5 mm (¼ inch) thick. Cut out Christmas tree shapes from thick card about 9 cm (3½ inches) high or use a metal cutter and cut out as many 'trees' as possible, rerolling the pastry trimmings.

Place the 'trees' on the baking sheets and mark the branches with the prongs of a fork. Brush lightly with egg white and bake in the centre of the oven for 10–15 minutes until a pale brown. Cool on a wire rack.

The biscuits may be lightly dredged with icing sugar to represent snow. Store in an airtight container.

# PINEAPPLE BUTTONS

Makes about 20 pairs

*100 g (4 oz) butter*
*2 tbsp double cream*
*100 g (4 oz) plain flour*
*caster sugar*
*50 g (2 oz) butter*
*100 g (4 oz) icing sugar, sifted*
*1 egg yolk*
*50 g (2 oz) glacé pineapple, finely chopped*

Prepare two ungreased baking sheets. Heat the oven to 190°C (375°F) mark 5. Cream the butter until very soft, then beat in the cream. Sift the flour and work into the mixture. Wrap in cling film or foil and chill for at least an hour.

Roll out the dough lightly on a floured board to about 3 mm (⅛ inch) thick. Cut into plain rounds using a 4-cm (1½-inch) cutter. Dredge both sides with sugar and place on the ungreased baking sheets. Prick with a fork and bake in the centre of the oven for about 10 minutes or until slightly puffy, but not browned. Cool on a wire rack.

For the filling: cream the butter and icing sugar until soft then beat in the egg yolk and glacé pineapple. Use to sandwich the biscuits together in pairs.

# ORANGE MELTAWAYS

Makes about 40

*225 g (8 oz) butter*
*50 g (2 oz) icing sugar, sifted*
*grated rind of 1 orange*
*225 g (8 oz) plain flour, sifted*
*4 tbsp apricot jam, sieved*
*1 tbsp water*
*2 tbsp icing sugar, sifted*
*a little orange or lemon juice*

Grease two or three baking sheets. Heat the oven to 160°C (325°F) mark 3. Cream the butter until soft then add the icing sugar and beat together until blended. Beat in the orange rind then work in the flour. Place the mixture in a large piping bag fitted with a large star nozzle. Pipe about 40 shell shapes on to the baking sheets and chill for 30 minutes.

Bake for about 25 minutes or until slightly coloured. Remove from the oven and brush each cookie first with apricot glaze (apricot jam heated with water) and then with the icing sugar blended with a little orange juice to make a soft icing. Return to the oven for 5 minutes.

# FRUITED GINGER BISCUITS

Makes 35–40

*100 g (4 oz) butter or margarine*
*100 g (4 oz) demerara sugar*
*200 g (8 oz) plain flour*
*2 tsp ground ginger*
*1 tsp ground cinnamon*
*1 tsp bicarbonate of soda*
*50 g (2 oz) golden syrup, warmed*
*75 g (3 oz) currants*
*about 3 tbsp milk*
*blanched almonds*

Grease two baking sheets. Heat the oven to 180°C (350°F) mark 4.

Cream the butter and sugar until light and fluffy. Sift together the flour, ginger, cinnamon and soda. Stir into the creamed mixture followed by the syrup, currants and sufficient milk to give a fairly soft dough.

Place teaspoons of the mixture on the baking sheets allowing plenty of room for them to spread. Place a blanched almond on each one and bake just above the centre of the oven for about 20 minutes or until well risen and browned.

Cool slightly on the baking sheet before removing carefully to a wire rack to cool. Store in an airtight container.

# COCONUT WAFERS

Makes about 15

*90 g (3½ oz) butter*
*100 g (4 oz) caster sugar*
*25 g (1 oz) long-shred coconut, roughly chopped*
*25 g (1 oz) angelica, roughly chopped*
*1 tsp flour*
*1 tbsp top of the milk*

Line two baking sheets with non-stick parchment. Heat the oven to 180°C (350°F) mark 4.

Melt the butter in a small pan, add the sugar and boil for a minute or so stirring continuously. Remove from the heat and stir in the coconut, angelica, flour and milk.

Cool a little, then drop in small heaps well apart on to the baking sheets. Bake just above the centre of the oven for about 10 minutes or until golden brown.

Leave briefly until they begin to firm up and then lay over a greased rolling pin and leave until cold and firm. Repeat with the remaining mixture.

Store in an airtight container for up to a week.

# BISCUITS WITH CHOCOLATE

The flavour of chocolate is many people's favourite. The biscuits and cookies here are all flavoured with chocolate in one way or another. Some are dipped or topped with chocolate, some have a chocolate filling, while others are made from a chocolate-flavoured dough.

# CATHERINE WHEELS

Makes about 24

*75 g (3 oz) butter*
*100 g (4 oz) caster sugar*
*½ egg*
*175 g (6 oz) plain flour*
*½ tsp baking powder*
*pinch of salt*
*1 tbsp cocoa powder*
*1 tsp milk*
*½ tsp vanilla essence*

Heat the oven to 160°C (325°F) mark 3. Cream the butter and 75 g (3 oz) of the sugar until light and fluffy. Gradually beat in the egg. Sift together the flour, baking powder and salt then fold into the creamed mixture to make a soft dough. Divide the dough into two equal parts. Add the sifted cocoa and milk to one portion and work it in gently with the fingertips. Add the essence to the other portion.

Roll each piece into an oblong 25 x 15 cm (10 x 6 inches). Place the cocoa dough on top of the plain dough and roll up the two layers closely and firmly from one long side. Wrap the roll in foil or cling film and chill in the refrigerator for 30 minutes.

Grease two baking sheets. Cut the dough into 24 slices and place on the baking sheets. Bake in the centre of the oven for 15–20 minutes or until golden brown. Cool on a wire rack before dredging with the remaining caster sugar.

# CHOCOLATE CHIP BISCUITS

*100 g (4 oz) butter*
*100 g (4 oz) caster sugar*
*2 tbsp condensed milk*
*75 g (3 oz) plain chocolate*
*175 g (6 oz) self-raising flour*

Heat the oven to 150°C (300°F) mark 2. Cream the butter and sugar together until light and fluffy, then beat in the condensed milk. Break or chop the chocolate into chips the size of sultanas and add to the creamed ingredients. Sift the flour and work into the mixture. Mix the dough well, then roll into walnut-sized balls.

Place on greased baking sheets and press down with a fork. Bake for 25–30 minutes or until golden brown. Cool on a wire rack.

# DROP COOKIES

*175 g (6 oz) plain flour*
*1 tsp bicarbonate of soda*
*pinch of salt*
*100 g (4 oz) butter or margarine*
*75 g (3 oz) caster sugar*
*25 g (1 oz) soft brown sugar*
*1 egg*
*a few drops of vanilla essence*
*100 g (4 oz) chocolate chips*

Heat the oven to 160°C (325°F) mark 3. Sift together the flour, soda and salt. Cream the butter and both of the sugars in a basin until they are light and fluffy. Gradually beat in the light beaten egg and vanilla essence. Stir in half of the flour mixture, beat well to give a smooth dough, then add the remaining flour and the chocolate chips. Blend to form a smooth dough.

Take rounded teaspoons of the mixture and place on greased baking sheets – about 12 to a sheet. Bake for 12–15 minutes then lift care fully on to a wire rack so that they lie flat. Store the biscuits in an airtight container when cold.

# CARAMEL BISCUITS

*100 g (4 oz) butter*
*50 g (2 oz) caster sugar*
*175 g (6 oz) self-raising flour, sifted*

Caramel
*200-g (7-oz) can condensed milk*
*100 g (4 oz) margarine*
*50 g (2 oz) caster sugar*
*2 tbsp golden syrup*
*a few drops of vanilla essence*

Topping
*200 g (7 oz) chocolate (plain or milk)*

Heat the oven to 180°C (350°F) mark 4. For the base: cream the butter and sugar until light and fluffy then mix in the flour. Press the dough into a greased rectangular tin 30 x 20 cm (12 x 8 inches) and bake for 15 minutes until golden brown. Leave to cool in the tin.

For the caramel: put all the ingredients in a pan and melt over a gentle heat. Bring to the boil and boil the mixture for 5 minutes, stirring all the time. Cool until it begins to thicken then pour over the base and leave to set.

For the topping: melt the chocolate in a basin over a pan of hot water and pour over the caramel. As it sets, swirl the top with a round-bladed knife. When quite set, cut into fingers.

# CHOCOLATE BISCUITS

Makes about 24

*75 g (3 oz) butter*
*175 g (6 oz) caster sugar*
*1 egg*
*1 tsp vanilla essence*
*175 g (6 oz) self-raising flour*
*1 tbsp cocoa powder*
*chocolate (plain or milk)*

Heat the oven to 190°C (375°F) mark 5. Cream the butter and sugar until light and fluffy. Add the egg and vanilla essence and beat again. Sift the flour and cocoa together and work into the mixture.

Roll teaspoons of the dough into balls, place on a greased baking sheet and flatten slightly. Bake for about 15 minutes, then cool on a wire rack.

When the biscuits are cold, top with melted chocolate and leave to set.

# COCONUT AND CHERRY SLICES

*150 g (5 oz) cooking chocolate*
*50 g (2 oz) margarine*
*100 g (4 oz) caster sugar*
*1 egg*
*50 g (2 oz) glacé cherries*
*100 g (4 oz) desiccated coconut*

Heat the oven to 170°C (335°F) mark 3–4. Line a Swiss roll tin with foil. Melt the chocolate in a bowl over a pan of hot water and then spread it over the foil and leave to cool.

Cream the margarine and sugar until light and fluffy then beat in the egg. Chop the cherries and fold in to the creamed mixture with the coconut. Spread this mixture over the cooled chocolate and bake for 15–20 minutes. Leave to cool in the tin and when the biscuit is cold, cut into slices. Store in an airtight container.

# CHOCOLATE PEPPERMINT CREAMS

*100 g (4 oz) butter*
*50 g (2 oz) caster sugar*
*½ tsp baking powder*
*1 tbsp drinking chocolate*
*100 g (4 oz) plain flour*
*75 g (3 oz) desiccated coconut*

Filling
*75 g (3 oz) butter*
*75 g (3 oz) icing sugar*
*¼ tsp peppermint essence*
*drop of green food colouring*

Topping
*100 g (4 oz) cooking chocolate*

Heat the oven to 190°C (375°F) mark 5. For the base: cream the butter and sugar until light and fluffy. Sift the baking powder, drinking chocolate and flour together and add to the creamed mixture with the coconut. Press the mixture into a Swiss roll tin lined with greased greaseproof paper. Bake for about 15–20 minutes on the middle shelf of the oven until an even colour all over. Leave in the tin to cool.

For the filling: cream the butter and sugar until light and creamy then add the essence and colouring. Spread it evenly over the base.

Cover the layer of filling with the melted cooking chocolate and leave to set. Cut the biscuit into squares or fingers when the chocolate is firm.

# CHOCOLATE QUICKIES

Makes 12–16

*100 g (4 oz) butter or margarine*
*2 tbsp cocoa powder*
*1 tbsp demerara sugar*
*2 tbsp golden syrup*
*225 g (8 oz) semi-sweet biscuits, crushed*
*100 g (4 oz) plain or milk chocolate, broken up*

Grease an 18-cm (7-inch) shallow square cake tin. Melt the butter in a small pan. Add the cocoa, sugar and syrup and when melted bring up to the boil. Boil for 1 minute. Remove from the heat and stir in the biscuit crumbs.

Turn the mixture into the tin and press in well to give a smooth top. Melt the chocolate in a basin over a pan of hot water, beat until smooth, then pour over the biscuit mixture. As the chocolate sets mark it into swirls with a round-bladed knife.

Chill until set firmly and then cut into squares or bars.

# CHOCOLATE STARS

*225 g (8 oz) plain flour*
*25 g (1 oz) cornflour*
*15 g (½ oz) cocoa powder*
*pinch of salt*
*100 g (4 oz) butter*
*100 g (4 oz) caster sugar*
*1 egg*
*½ tsp vanilla essence*
*2 tsp milk*
*50 g (2 oz) chococlate drops*

Heat the oven to 160°C (325°F) mark 3. Sift the flour, cornflour, cocoa and salt into a bowl. Cream the butter and sugar until they are light and fluffy. Beat in the egg and vanilla essence. Work in the flour mixture and mix to a soft dough with the milk.

Put the mixture into a large forcing bag fitted with a large star nozzle. Pipe stars 4 cm (1½ inches) in diameter, spaced well apart, on greased baking sheets. Place a chocolate drop in the centre of each star and bake in the centre of the oven for 15 minutes. Cool on a wire rack.

# CURLY PETERS

Plain mixture
*100 g (4 oz) margarine*
*225 g (8 oz) plain flour, sifted*
*100 g (4 oz) caster sugar*
*1 tsp baking powder*
*1 egg, beaten*

Chocolate mixture
*100 g (4 oz) margarine*
*175 g (6 oz) plain flour, sifted with 50 g (2 oz) cocoa powder*
*100 g (4 oz) caster sugar*
*1 tsp baking powder*
*1 egg, beaten*

Heat the oven to 150–160°C (300–325°F) mark 2–3. For both mixtures: rub the margarine into the flour until the mixture resembles fine breadcrumbs, then add the sugar and baking powder. Bind them together with the egg to make a stiff dough.

Roll out each mixture separately on a floured board to the same size, then lay the chocolate mixture on top of the plain one. Roll up like a Swiss roll and cut the roll into 5-mm (¼-inch) slices. Lay on greased baking sheets and bake for 20–25 minutes or until pale brown. Cool on a wire rack.

# CHOCOLATE CHERRY BISCUITS

Makes 18–20

*100 g (4 oz) softened butter*
*50 g (2 oz) caster sugar*
*½ tsp vanilla essence*
*25 g (1 oz) glacé cherries*
*25 g (1 oz) plain chococlate*
*100 g (4 oz) plain flour, sifted*

Heat the oven to 190°C (375°F) mark 5. Cream the butter and sugar until light and fluffy and then add the vanilla essence. Chop the cherries and the chocolate finely and add to the mixture; finally, work in the flour.

Place 18–20 teaspoons of the mixture on well greased baking sheets leaving space for the biscuits to spread. Bake for 15–20 minutes then cool on a wire rack.

# CHERRY AND CHOCOLATE CHEWS

Makes 35

*100 g (4 oz) butter*
*50 g (2 oz) caster sugar*
*2 tbsp condensed milk*
*175 g (6 oz) self-raising flour*
*pinch of salt*
*75 g (3 oz) plain cooking chocolate*
*50 g (2 oz) glacé cherries*

Heat the oven to 180°C (350°F) mark 4. Cream the butter and sugar until light and fluffy then beat in the milk. Sift in the flour and salt. Chop the chocolate and cherries into small pieces and fold through the mixture.

Take good teaspoons of the mixture and roll into balls. Place on a greased baking sheet and flatten slightly. Bake for about 25 minutes. Cool on a wire rack.

# CHOCOLATE WAGON WHEELS

*100 g (4 oz) plain flour*
*pinch of salt*
*50 g (2 oz) margarine*
*25 g (1 oz) caster sugar*
*a few drops of vanilla essence*
*a little egg*
*25 g (1 oz) chocolate (plain or milk)*

Heat the oven to 200°C (400°F) mark 6. Sift the flour and salt into a bowl and rub in the margarine until the mixture resembles fine breadcrumbs. Add the sugar and essence and mix to a dough with the beaten egg.

Roll the dough out on a lightly floured board and cut into 5-cm (2-inch) rounds with a plain cutter. Place on greased baking sheets and bake for about 10 minutes. Cool on a wire rack.

When the biscuits are cold, melt the chocolate over a pan of hot water. Dip each biscuit half-way into the chocolate and smooth its surface with a knife. Leave to set on a wire rack.

# ICED PEPPERMINT BISCUITS

*75 g (3 oz) plain flour*
*50 g (2 oz) butter*
*25 g (1 oz) sugar*

Icing
*a few drops of peppermint essence*
*a few drops of green food colouring*
*about 1 tbsp water*
*100 g (4 oz) icing sugar*

Topping
*225 g (8 oz) cooking chocolate*
*chocolate vermicelli*

Heat the oven to 160°C (325°F) mark 3. Sift the flour into a bowl, rub in the butter until the mixture resembles breadcrumbs, then add the sugar. Knead until the mixture is smooth. Roll out thinly on a lightly floured board and cut into shapes. Place the biscuits on a greased baking sheet and bake for 10–15 minutes. Allow to cool before removing them from the baking sheet to a wire rack.

Prepare the icing by adding the peppermint essence and food colouring to the water. Mix in the sifted icing sugar and beat to a smooth consistency. Not all the water may be required as the icing should be quite thick. Spread the biscuits with the icing and leave to set.

Melt the chocolate over hot water and use to coat the biscuits, then decorate with the vermicelli. Leave to set.

# QUICK FLORENTINES

*175 g (6 oz) dates, chopped*
*50 g (2 oz) sultanas*
*100 g (4 oz) margarine*
*50 g (2 oz) caster sugar*
*50 g (2 oz) glacé cherries, chopped*
*25 g (1 oz) crystallized ginger, finely chopped*
*65 g (2½ oz) rice crispies*
*225 g (8 oz) cooking chocolate*

Put the dates and sultanas in a saucepan with the margarine. Heat slowly, stirring all the time until soft. Add the sugar, cherries, ginger and rice crispies and stir well. Press the mixture into a Swiss roll tin and leave to set until firm.

Melt the chocolate in a bowl over hot water, and spread over the cooled mixture. Leave to set, then cut into bars.

# CHOCOLATE MUESLI BISCUITS

*75 g (3 oz) margarine*
*1 tbsp golden syrup*
*225 g (8 oz) muesli*
*50 g (2 oz) dates, chopped*
*50 g (2 oz) glacé cherries*
*100 g (4 oz) cooking chocolate*

Melt the margarine and golden syrup together in a saucepan. Remove from the heat and stir in the muesli, dates and cherries. Press the mixture into a Swiss roll tin and leave to set.

Melt the chocolate in a bowl over hot water, and spread it over the cooled biscuit mixture. When set, cut into bars.

# CHOCOLATE COCONUT KISSES

*2 egg whites*
*100 g (4 oz) icing sugar*
*50 g (2 oz) desiccated coconut*
*100 g (4 oz) bitter chocolate, chopped*

Heat the oven to 150°C (300°F) mark 2. Beat the egg whites stiffly, then add the icing sugar a little at a time, beating after each addition. Fold in the coconut and chocolate chips. Bake on an oiled baking sheet or a baking sheet lined with non-stick parchment, placing the mixture in small heaps.

Cook for 30 minutes until crisp.

# GIPSY CREAMS

*50 g (2 oz) lard*
*50 g (2 oz) margarine*
*50 g (2 oz) caster sugar*
*100 g (4 oz) self-raising flour, sifted*
*50 g (2 oz) rolled oats*
*1 tbsp chocolate or cocoa powder*
*2 tsp golden syrup dissolved in 1 tbsp hot water*

Filling
*25 g (1 oz) butter*
*50 g (2 oz) icing sugar*
*1 tbsp chocolate powder*
*a few drops of vanilla essence*

Heat the oven to 180°C (350°F) mark 4. For the biscuits: cream the lard, margarine and sugar until light and fluffy, then mix in all the other ingredients. Roll the dough into balls about the size of a large cherry.

Place on greased baking sheets and flatten with a fork which has been dipped in water. Bake for about 20 minutes, and leave on the baking sheets to cool.

To make the filling: cream the butter until it is soft. Gradually add the sifted icing sugar and beat until smooth. Add the chocolate powder and vanilla essence and beat well.

When the biscuits are cold, sandwich together in pairs with the filling.

# OAT BISCUITS

Rolled oats add a delicious flavour and crunchiness to biscuits and cookies. Many of these recipes are made by melting the fat with sugar or syrup and kneading in the other ingredients. The biscuits are all crisp, crunchy and very 'moreish'.

# ROLLED OAT BISCUITS

*225 g (8 oz) butter or margarine*
*100 g (4 oz) soft brown sugar*
*175 g (6 oz) plain flour*
*75 g (3 oz) rolled oats*
*pinch of bicarbonate of soda*
*pinch of salt*

Heat the oven to 150°C (300°F) mark 2. Cream the butter and sugar until soft then work in all the other ingredients. Roll the dough out on a floured board, but do not make it too thin. Cut into shapes and place on greased baking sheets. Cook for 20–25 minutes until golden brown. Cool on a wire rack.

# COUPLAND BISCUITS

*100 g (4 oz) butter or margarine*
*50 g (2 oz) caster sugar*
*1 tbsp golden syrup*
*100 g (4 oz) plain flour*
*50 g (2 oz) rolled oats*
*50 g (2 oz) desiccated coconut*
*1 tsp bicarbonate of soda*
*2 tsp hot water*

Heat the oven to 180°C (350°F) mark 4. Beat the butter, sugar and syrup together until they are soft and creamy. Sift the flour and add to the mixture with the oats, coconut and the soda blended in the water; mix together to form a dough.

Roll the dough into small balls, place on greased baking sheets and flatten with a round-bladed knife. Bake for about 20 minutes or until golden brown. Cool on a wire rack.

# OAT BISCUITS

*100 g (4 oz) plain flour*
*1 tsp bicarbonate of soda*
*100 g (4 oz) rolled oats*
*100 g (4 oz) butter*
*100 g (4 oz) caster sugar*
*1 tbsp golden syrup*
*1 tbsp water*

Heat the oven to 180°C (350°F) mark 4. Sift the flour and soda into a bowl and mix in the oats. Dissolve the butter, sugar and syrup in the water over a low heat, then stir into the dry ingredients.

Put teaspoons of the mixture on very well greased baking sheets, leaving room for the biscuits to spread. Bake on the top shelf of the oven for 15–20 minutes. Leave to cool for only a few seconds, then loosen with a palette knife. Cool on a wire rack.

# TEBAY CRUNCH

*225 g (8 oz) butter*
*100 g (4 oz) caster sugar*
*350 g (12 oz) rolled oats*

Heat the oven to 180°C (350°F) mark 4. Heat the butter and sugar in a pan until melted, then add the oats gradually and mix well together.

Turn the mixture into a greased rectangular tin approximately 28 x 18 cm (11 x 7 inches) and bake for 15–20 minutes until lightly browned. Leave in the tin to cool. Cut into pieces when cold.

# BLANTYRE BISCUITS

*100 g (4 oz) butter or margarine*
*100 g (4 oz) caster sugar*
*100 g (4 oz) rolled oats*
*100 g (4 oz) wholemeal flour*
*½ tsp baking powder*
*1 egg, beaten*
*2 bananas or 75 g (3 oz) chopped nuts*

Heat the oven to 180°C (350°F) mark 4. Cream the butter and sugar until light and fluffy. Mix in the oats, flour and baking powder. Add the egg and divide the dough into two portions.

Put one half into a greased, shallow 20-cm (8-inch) square tin and press it down with a fork. Spread the sliced bananas or nuts over this and cover with the remaining dough. Press it down firmly. Bake for 15–20 minutes or until golden brown. Cut into fingers. Cool in the tin then remove when cold and break up into fingers.

# FIRELIGHTER BISCUITS

*100 g (4 oz) margarine*
*1 tbsp golden syrup*
*225 g (8 oz) rolled oats*
*100 g (4 oz) brown sugar*
*25 g (1 oz) desiccated coconut*
*pinch of baking powder*

Heat the oven to 180°C (350°F) mark 4. Melt the fat and syrup together in a pan, add the dry ingredients and mix together thoroughly. Press the dough into a greased Swiss roll tin so that it is 1 cm (½ inch) thick. Bake for 20–30 minutes. Leave in the tin and cut into fingers when it is cold.

# CUMBERLAND SNAPS

*100 g (4 oz) caster sugar*
*225 g (8 oz) margarine*
*2 tbsp golden syrup*
*1 tsp bicarbonate of soda*
*1 tbsp hot water*
*225 g (8 oz) plain flour*
*1 tsp ground ginger*
*50 g (2 oz) rolled oats*

Heat the oven to 160°C (325°F) mark 3. Melt the sugar, margarine and syrup in a pan over a low heat. Dissolve the soda in the hot water. Sift the flour and ginger together and then mix together with all the other ingredients.

Roll the dough into small balls about the size of a walnut and place on greased baking sheets. Bake for 20–25 minutes until golden brown. Cool on a wire rack.

# BUTTERCRUNCH

*225 g (8 oz) self-raising flour*
*pinch of salt*
*175 g (6 oz) butter*
*2 tbsp golden syrup*
*175 g (6 oz) demerara sugar*
*100 g (4 oz) rolled oats*

Heat the oven to 180°C (350°F) mark 4. Sift the flour and salt into a bowl and rub in the butter until the mixture resembles fine breadcrumbs. Add the syrup, sugar and oats and mix to form a firm dough. Break off pieces of dough the size of a walnut and roll into balls.

Place on greased baking sheets and flatten slightly. Bake for 15–20 minutes then cool on a wire rack.

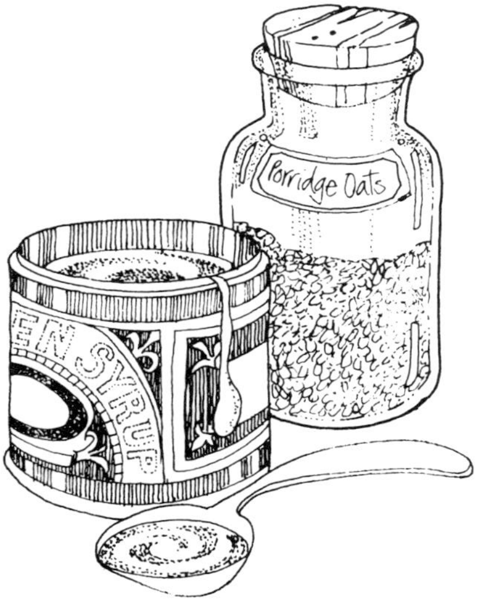

# ABBEY BISCUITS

Makes about 24

*150 g (5 oz) margarine*
*150 g (5 oz) caster sugar*
*1 tbsp milk*
*1 tsp bicarbonate of soda*
*1 tsp golden syrup*
*150 g (5 oz) plain flour, sifted*
*100 g (4 oz) rolled oats*

Heat the oven to 150°C (300°F) mark 2. Cream the margarine and sugar together, then add the milk, soda and syrup. Stir in the flour and oats and mix well. Roll the dough into small balls and space evenly apart on lightly greased baking sheets. Bake for 25 minutes until goden brown. Cool on a wire rack.

# FLAKED ALMOND BISCUITS

Makes 48

*100 g (4 oz) butter or margarine*
*100 g (4 oz) caster sugar*
*2 tsp black treacle*
*100 g (4 oz) self-raising flour, sifted*
*100 g (4 oz) rolled oats*
*25 g (1 oz) flaked almonds*
*1 tsp bicarbonate of soda*
*4 tbsp boiling water*

Heat the oven to 180°C (350°F) mark 4. Cream the butter and sugar until light and fluffy. Add the treacle, then mix in the flour, oats and almonds. Dissolve the soda in the water and stir into the mixture to form a dough.

Roll teaspoons of the mixture into balls and place on greased baking sheets, allowing room for the biscuits to spread. Bake for 15 minutes. Cool on a wire rack.

# CRUNCHIES

*1 tsp bicarbonate of soda*
*1 tbsp tepid water*
*100 g (4 oz) margarine*
*1 tbsp golden syrup*
*100 g (4 oz) self-raising flour, sifted*
*100 g (4 oz) rolled oats*
*100 g (4 oz) granulated sugar*
*100 g (4 oz) desiccated coconut*

Heat the oven to 150°C (300°F) mark 2. Dissolve the soda in the water. Melt the fat and syrup in a pan and then mix all the ingredients together to form a dough.

Roll the dough into small balls and place on greased baking sheets. Bake for about 20 minutes. Cool on a wire rack.

# PEPPERMINT OAT BISCUITS

*100 g (4 oz) lard*
*100 g (4 oz) margarine*
*2 tsp golden syrup*
*175 g (6 oz) sugar*
*¼ tsp bicarbonate of soda*
*4 tsp boiling water*
*225 g (8 oz) plain flour, sifted*
*225 g (8 oz) rolled oats*
*1 tsp baking powder*
*2 tsp vanilla essence*

Filling
*75 g (3 oz) butter*
*175 g (6 oz) icing sugar*
*a few drops of peppermint essence*

Heat the oven to 200°C (400°F) mark 6. To make the biscuits: cream the lard, margarine, syrup and sugar until light and fluffy. Dissolve the soda in the boiling water and add to the creamed mixture together with all the other ingredients and work to form a dough. Roll out the dough on a lightly floured board and cut into rounds. Place on well greased baking sheets and bake for 15–20 minutes or until pale brown. Cool on a wire rack.

For the filling: cream the butter until it is soft. Gradually add the sifted icing sugar and cream together. Add the peppermint essence to taste and beat thoroughly.

When the biscuits are cold, sandwich together with the filling.

# CHOCOLATE OAT BISCUITS

*100 g (4 oz) self-raising flour*
*100 g (4 oz) rolled oats*
*75 g (3 oz) caster sugar*
*50 g (2 oz) lard*
*50 g (2 oz) margarine*
*1 tsp golden syrup*
*1 tsp bicarbonate of soda*
*1 tsp vanilla essence*
*1 tbsp boiling water*

Filling
*50 g (2 oz) butter*
*100 g (4 oz) icing sugar*
*1 tbsp cocoa powder*

Topping
*cooking chocolate (plain or milk)*

Heat the oven to 180°C (350°F) mark 4. For the biscuits: mix the sifted flour, oats and sugar together in a bowl, then rub in the lard and margarine. Mix the remaining ingredients together and add to the dry ingredients to make a fairly soft dough. Knead the dough into a ball, wrap in cling film or foil, and chill for 30 minutes.

Roll the dough out on a floured board and cut into 6-cm (2-inch) rounds then place on greased baking sheets. Bake for about 20 minutes. Cool on a wire rack.

For the filling: cream the butter until it is soft. Add the sifted icing sugar and cream together. Add the cocoa and beat well.

Sandwich the biscuits together in pairs with the filling and coat the tops with melted chocolate.

# BUFTON BISCUITS

*150 g (5 oz) margarine*
*100 g (4 oz) granulated sugar*
*100 g (4 oz) self-raising flour*
*1 tsp baking powder*
*25 g (1 oz) semolina*
*100 g (4 oz) rolled oats*
*2 tbsp golden syrup*
*pinch of salt*
*1 tsp bicarbonate of soda*
*2 tsp milk*

Filling
*50 g (2 oz) butter*
*100 g (4 oz) icing sugar*
*1 tsp cocoa powder*
*1 tsp coffee essence*

Heat the oven to 180°C (350°F) mark 4. For the biscuits: cream the margarine and sugar together until soft and creamy. Sift the flour and baking powder together and add with the semolina, oats, syrup and salt to the creamed mixture. Lastly, add the soda mixed with the milk. Mix to form a smooth dough.

Shape into small, rough balls and place on a greased baking sheet. Bake for 15–20 minutes until they are set. Cool on a wire rack.

To make the filling: cream the butter until it is soft. Gradually add the sifted icing sugar, and cream together. Add the cocoa powder and coffee essence and beat the mixture well. When the biscuits are cold, sandwich them together with this mocha butter cream.

# ANZAC COOKIES

*175 g (6 oz) butter*
*1 tsp golden syrup*
*1 tsp bicarbonate of soda*
*2 tbsp boiling water*
*100 g (4 oz) plain flour, sifted*
*100 g (4 oz) rolled oats*
*175 g (6 oz) caster sugar*
*100 g (4 oz) raisins, chopped*

Heat the oven to 150°C (300°F) mark 2. Melt the butter and syrup in a pan. Dissolve the soda in the water and add this to the butter. Mix together the flour, oats, sugar and raisins in a bowl and pour in the liquid. Mix thoroughly to form a dough.

Place teaspoons of the mixture on greased baking sheets, allowing room for spreading. Bake for about 15 minutes. Remove the biscuits carefully and cool on a wire rack.

# MELTING MOMENTS

Makes 24

*100 g (4 oz) butter*
*100 g (4 oz) caster sugar*
*1 egg*
*175 g (6 oz) self-raising flour, sifted*
*pinch of salt*
*50 g (2 oz) rolled oats*
*12 glacé cherries*

Heat the oven to 180°C (350°F) mark 4. Beat the butter until it is soft and creamy. Add the sugar, and cream until the mixture is light and fluffy and drops easily from the spoon. Beat in the egg with 25 g (1 oz) of the flour. Fold in the remaining flour and the salt, and mix to form a stiff dough.

Divide the mixture into 24 pieces and, with wet hands, roll each one into a ball. Roll the balls in the oats and place on greased baking sheets, allowing room to spread. Flatten each one slightly and place half a glacé cherry in the centre of each biscuit. Bake for 20 minutes. Allow to set a little on the baking sheets then remove to a wire rack and leave until cold.

# DATE SLICES

*100 g (4 oz) stoned dates, chopped*
*100 g (4 oz) self-raising flour*
*100 g (4 oz) butter or margarine*
*100 g (4 oz) caster sugar*
*100 g (4 oz) rolled oats*

Heat the oven to 180°C (350°F) mark 4. Simmer the dates with sufficient water to barely cover them until the mixture resembles thick jam. More water may be added or boiled off if necessary.

Sift the flour, and rub in fat until the mixture resembles breadcrumbs, then mix in the sugar and oats and knead together. Press half of this mixture into a greased Swiss roll tin, spread the dates on top, and cover with the remainder of the dough.

Bake for about 20 minutes or until the surface is evenly browned. Cut into fingers while it is still hot, but leave in the tin until cool and firm.

# NUT BISCUITS

In this chapter, walnuts, peanuts, almonds and other nuts are used to flavour, decorate or add texture to a selection of biscuits. Many use nuts which are interchangeable, so you can vary the flavours and textures as you please.

# WALNUT BARS

*225 g (8 oz) butter*
*225 g (8 oz) caster sugar*
*1 egg, separated*
*1 tsp vanilla essence*
*200 g (7 oz) plain flour, sifted*
*50 g (2 oz) shelled walnuts, chopped*

Heat the oven to 180°C (350°F) mark 4. Cream the butter and sugar together until light and fluffy. Beat in the egg yolk, vanilla essence and the flour. Press the mixture into a greased rectangular tin 25 x 18 x 5 cm (10 x 7 x 2 inches).

Lightly whisk the egg white and brush it over the dough. Sprinkle on the walnuts and bake for 45 minutes. Cool in the tin and cut into bars as it cools.

# DATE STICKS

*2 eggs*
*50 g (2 oz) caster sugar*
*pinch of salt*
*25 g (1 oz) butter, melted*
*450 g (1 lb) stoned dates, chopped*
*50 g (2 oz) shelled walnuts, chopped*
*175 g (6 oz) self-raising flour, sifted*
*1 tbsp hot water*
*caster sugar to sprinkle*

Heat the oven to 190°C (375°F) mark 5. Beat together the eggs, sugar, salt and melted butter. Mix in the dates and walnuts, then add the flour and hot water. Work to a dough.

Spread the mixture into two well greased and floured Swiss roll tins. Bake for 20–25 minutes. Cut into fingers and sprinkle with caster sugar whilst hot, then leave in the tins until cold before removing.

# WALNUT CRISPS

*225 g (8 oz) self-raising flour*
*75 g (3 oz) margarine*
*25 g (1 oz) butter*
*225 g (8 oz) soft brown sugar*
*100 g (4 oz) plain chocolate*
*100 g (4 oz) shelled walnuts, roughly chopped*
*1 egg, beaten*

Heat the oven to 180°C (350°F) mark 4. Sift the flour into a bowl and rub in the margarine until the mixture resembles fine breadcrumbs. Mix in the sugar. Break the chocolate into small pieces and add to the dry ingredients together with the walnuts. Bind the mixture together with the egg.

Place small heaps of the dough on greased baking sheets and flatten with a fork. Bake for about 25 minutes. Cool on a wire rack.

# COFFEE WALNUT BISCUITS

Makes about 20

*100 g (4 oz) plain flour*
*2 tsp instant coffee powder*
*100 g (4 oz) butter*
*50 g (2 oz) caster sugar*
*50 g (2 oz) shelled walnuts, chopped*

Heat the oven to 190°C (375°F) mark 5. Sift the flour and instant coffee together. Cream the butter and sugar together until light and fluffy, then add the rest of the ingredients. Place small teaspoons of the mixture on greased baking sheets leaving plenty of room for the biscuits to spread. Bake for 15–20 minutes. Cool on a wire rack.

# PEANUT COOKIES

*100 g (4 oz) soft margarine*
*100 g (4 oz) caster sugar*
*50 g (2 oz) salted peanuts*
*150 g (5 oz) self-raising flour*

Heat the oven to 180°C (350°F) mark 4. Cream the margarine and sugar together until light and fluffy. Chop the nuts and stir in the mixture with the sifted flour to make a dough. Shape into walnut-sized balls and place on greased baking sheets. Bake for about 20 minutes. Cool on a wire rack.

# ALMOND BUTTER CRISPS

Makes about 48

*200 g (7 oz) butter or margarine*
*175 g (6 oz) caster sugar*
*1 tsp vanilla essence*
*1 tsp bicarbonate of soda*
*225 g (8 oz) self-raising flour*
*about 48 split almonds*

Heat the oven to 180°C (350°F) mark 4. Work the butter into the sugar and when this has been absorbed, add the vanilla essence. Sift the soda with the flour and add to the other ingredients. Knead the dough until smooth.

Roll into balls the size of a walnut and place on lightly greased baking sheets leaving room for the biscuits to flatten and spread. Top each with a split almond. Bake for 15 minutes or until golden brown. Cool on a wire rack.

These light-as-air biscuits are often served in Denmark.

# HAZELNUT BISCUITS

*100 g (4 oz) butter*
*65 g (2½ oz) caster sugar*
*150 g (5 oz) plain flour, sifted*
*115 g (4½ oz) ground hazelnuts*
*a little honey*
*75 g (3 oz) plain block chocolate*

Heat the oven to 180°C (350°F) mark 4. Cream together the butter and sugar until light and fluffy. Stir the flour and 75 g (3 oz) of the ground hazelnuts into the mixture. Knead into a ball and roll out thinly. Cut into rounds using a 5-cm (2½-inch) cutter. Place the rounds on a greased baking sheet and bake for 12 minutes. Cool on a wire rack.

When cool, sandwich the rounds together with honey. Melt the chocolate in a bowl over hot water. Roll the edges of the biscuits in the melted chocolate and then in the remainder of the ground hazelnuts.

# NAPOLEON HATS

*50 g (2 oz) butter*
*50 g (2 oz) caster sugar*
*½ egg*
*100 g (4 oz) plain flour*
*pinch of baking powder*

Almond paste
*50 g (2 oz) icing sugar*
*25 g (1 oz) ground almonds*
*a little egg*

Icing
*50 g (2 oz) icing sugar*
*2 tsp water*

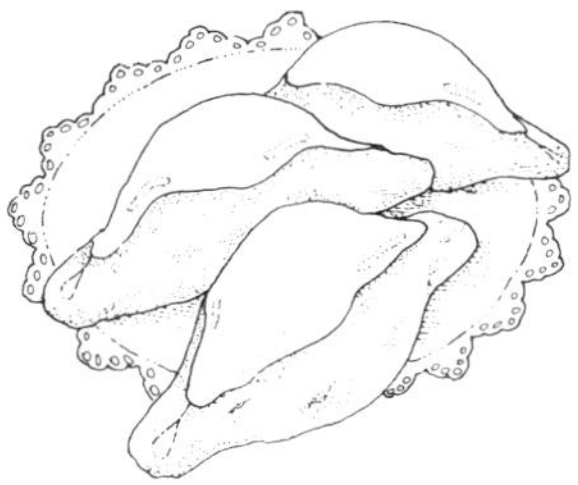

Heat the oven to 180°C (350°F) mark 4. To make the biscuits: cream the butter and sugar until light and fluffy. Beat in the egg and then mix to a stiff dough with the sifted flour and baking powder. Roll the dough out thinly and cut into rounds.

To make the almond paste: mix the icing sugar and ground almonds and add sufficient beaten egg to mix to a smooth consistency. Roll the almond paste into balls and place one on each biscuit. Fold up the two sides of the biscuits to make a shape like Napoleon's hat and place on greased baking sheets. Bake for about 20 minutes. Cool on a wire rack.

For the icing: mix the icing sugar with the water and beat until smooth. When the biscuits are cold, top each one with a little icing and leave to set.

# CHERRY SNOWBALLS

Makes about 36

*225 g (8 oz) butter*
*50 g (2 oz) icing sugar, sifted*
*225 g (8 oz) plain flour, sifted*
*pinch of salt*
*100 g (4 oz) shelled walnuts, chopped*
*1 tsp vanilla essence*
*glacé cherries*
*caster sugar for coating*

Heat the oven to 160°C (325°F) mark 3. Cream the butter with the icing sugar until light and fluffy. Add the rest of the ingredients except for the cherries to the creamed mixture and mix well.

Flatten teaspoons of the dough in the palms of your hands. Place a cherry on each round and cover it by pinching the dough up and around it. Roll into balls and place on a greased baking sheet.

Bake for 35 minutes. While still hot, roll the biscuits in caster sugar then cool on a wire rack.

# ALMOND BARS

Makes about 30

*225 g (8 oz) plain flour*
*150 g (6 oz) butter*
*100 g (4 oz) icing sugar, sifted*
*100 g (4 oz) blanched almonds, very finely chopped*
*1 egg white*
*2 tsp coffee essence*

Sift the flour on to a working surface and make a well in the centre. Cut the butter into pieces and put into the well with the sugar. Work the butter and sugar together with the fingertips, then gradually work in the flour. Finally work in the almonds and knead to a smooth dough. Wrap the dough in greaseproof paper and chill for 20–30 minutes.

Heat the oven to 190°C (375°F) mark 5. Grease two or three baking sheets. Using half the dough at a time, roll out to a rectangle about 5 mm (¼ inch) thick. Mark into a criss-cross pattern with a sharp knife. Mix the egg white and coffee essence together and brush all over the surface. Cut the dough into bars about 7.5 x 4 cm (3 x 1½ inches) and transfer carefully to the baking sheets. Repeat with the remaining dough.

Bake for about 15 minutes or until lightly coloured. Cool on a wire rack.

# NUT AND FRUIT SHORTBREAD

*175 g (6 oz) butter*
*75 g (3 oz) caster sugar*
*25 g (1 oz) ground rice*
*225 g (8 oz) plain flour*
*25 g (1 oz) glacé cherries, chopped*
*25 g (1 oz) angelica, chopped*
*50 g (2 oz) blanched almonds*

Heat the oven to 180°C (350°F) mark 4. Cream the butter and sugar until light and fluffy. Add the ground rice and sifted flour. Stir in the cherries, angelica and half the almonds and work to form a dough.

Place the dough in a greased 23-cm (9-inch) square cake tin and press the remainder of the almonds on the top. Bake for 30–40 minutes. Cool in the tin, marking into fingers when just firm.

# CHOCOLATE NUT BISCUITS

Makes about 50

*100 g (4 oz) butter*
*175 g (6 oz) caster sugar*
*1 egg, beaten*
*40 g (1½ oz) plain chocolate, grated*
*225 g (8 oz) plain flour, sifted*
*½ tsp cream of tartar*
*½ tsp bicarbonate of soda*
*pinch of salt*
*a few drops of vanilla essence*
*40 g (1½ oz) shelled walnuts, chopped*

Cream the butter until soft. Add the sugar and continue until light and fluffy. Add the egg, then the chocolate, together with all the other ingredients. Form the dough into a roll about 4 cm (1½ inches) in diameter, wrap in cling film or foil and chill until firm. Heat the oven to 180°C (350°F) mark 4.

Slice the roll thinly with a sharp knife. Place the rounds on greased baking sheets leaving room to spread. Bake for 10 minutes. Cool on a wire rack.

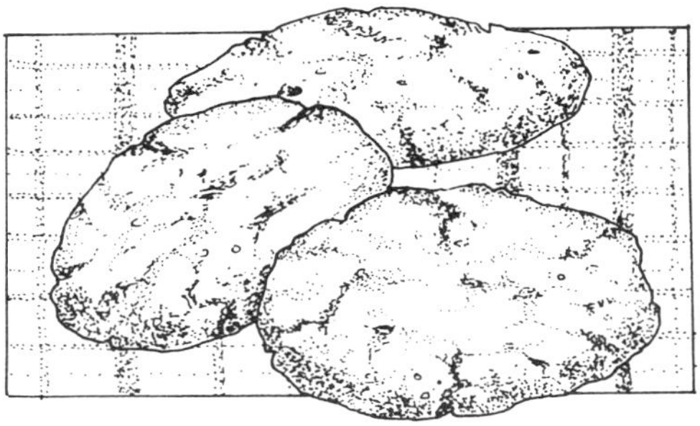

# LACE BISCUITS

*100 g (4 oz) margarine*
*100 g (4 oz) caster sugar*
*juice of 1 lemon*
*100 g (4 oz) chopped almonds*
*50 g (2 oz) plain flour*
*pinch of salt*

Heat the oven to 180°C (350°F) mark 4. Cream the margarine, sugar and lemon juice until light and fluffy. Add the almonds and then stir in the sifted flour and salt. Mix well to form a dough.

Break off pieces of dough the size of a walnut and place on greased baking sheets leaving room for the biscuits to spread. Press with a fork and bake for 15–20 minutes. Do not remove from the baking sheets until they are cold. Store in an airtight container.

# FRUITY BRITTLES

*100 g (4 oz) self-raising flour*
*pinch of salt*
*150 g (5 oz) butter or margarine*
*100 g (4 oz) caster sugar*
*100 g (4 oz) mixed dried fruit, chopped*
*50 g (2 oz) shelled walnuts, chopped*
*1 egg*
*100 g (4 oz) cornflakes, crushed*

Heat the oven to 200°C (400°F) mark 6. Sift the flour and salt into a bowl and rub in the butter until the mixture resembles breadcrumbs. Mix in the sugar, fruit and nuts. Beat the egg and work into the mixture.

Roll ping-pong ball sized pieces of the mixture in the crushed cornflakes. Place on greased baking sheets, leaving room for them to spread. Bake for 10–15 minutes. Cool on a wire rack.

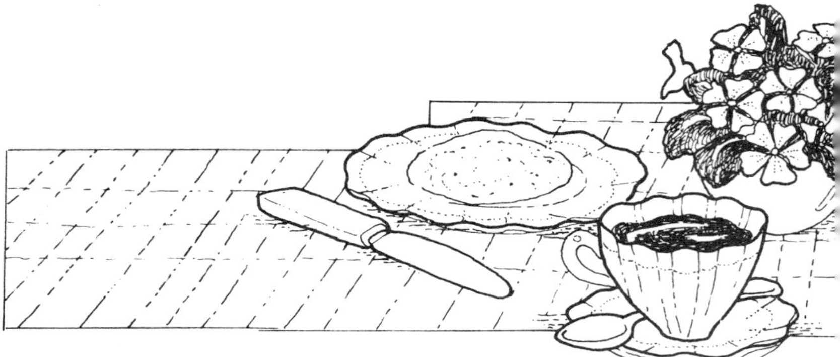

# CRESCENT BISCUITS

*200 g (7 oz) plain flour*
*75 g (3 oz) butter*
*75 g (3 oz) margarine*
*50 g (2 oz) caster sugar*
*75 g (3 oz) ground almonds*
*a few drops of vanilla essence*
*caster sugar for sprinkling*

Heat the oven to 150°C (300°F) mark 2. Sift the flour into a bowl and rub in the fats until the mixture resembles breadcrumbs. Add the sugar, almonds and essence and knead the mixture to form a stiff paste.

Roll the dough out on a floured board to a thickness of 1 cm (½ inch). Cut into crescent shapes using either a plain or a fluted cutter, and place on greased baking sheets. Bake for 30 minutes. Sprinkle with caster sugar and cool on a wire rack.

# CRESTON DROPS

*100 g (4 oz) butter*
*50 g (2 oz) caster sugar*
*2 eggs*
*3 squares chocolate, melted*
*100 g (4 oz) shelled walnuts, chopped*
*100 g (4 oz) raisins*
*225 g (8 oz) plain flour*
*1 tsp salt*
*½ tsp bicarbonate of soda*
*6 tbsp milk*

Heat the oven to 200°C (400°F) mark 6. Cream the butter and sugar together until light and fluffy. Beat in the eggs, then the melted chocolate, nuts and raisins. Sift the flour with the salt and soda and add them to the mixture alternating with the milk.

Drop teaspoons of the mixture on to greased baking sheets and flatten with a spoon. Bake for 10–15 minutes. Cool on a wire rack.

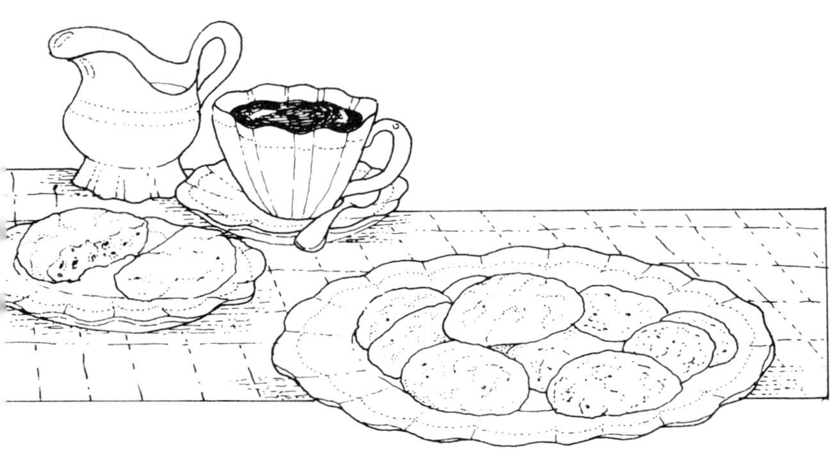

# KING HAAKON BISCUITS

*100 g (4 oz) icing sugar*
*pinch of salt*
*225 g (8 oz) plain flour*
*225 g (8 oz) butter*
*50 g (2 oz) shelled walnuts, chopped*
*50 g (2 oz) glacé cherries*

Heat the oven to 150°C (300°F) mark 2. Sift the icing sugar, salt and flour together and rub in the butter until the mixture resembles breadcrumbs. Add the other ingredients and form the dough into a good-shaped roll. Wrap in foil and put in the refrigerator until firm.

When the dough is very firm, cut into thin slices. Place on greased baking sheets and bake for 20–25 minutes. Cool on a wire rack.

# CARDAMOM COOKIES

Makes 30

*75 g (3 oz) icing sugar*
*225 g (8 oz) plain flour*
*225 g (8 oz) butter, softened*
*50 g (2 oz) shelled walnuts, chopped*
*1 tsp almond essence*
*½ tsp ground cardamom*
*pinch of salt*
*icing sugar to dredge*

Heat the oven to 180°C (350°F) mark 4. Sift the icing sugar and flour. Add the rest of the ingredients and work to give a firm mixture. Shape the dough into 2.5-cm (1-inch) balls and place 5 cm (2 inches) apart on greased baking sheets. Bake for 20 minutes or until golden brown. Cool on a wire rack. Dredge the cookies with icing sugar before serving.

# MARZIPAN BISCUITS

*100 g (4 oz) caster sugar*
*75 g (3 oz) ground almonds*
*finely grated rind of 1 small orange*
*2 small egg yolks*
*a few drops of almond essence*
*25 g (1 oz) flaked almonds*

Heat the oven to 190°C (375°F) mark 5. Mix the caster sugar, ground almonds and orange rind together in a medium-sized mixing bowl. Make a well in the centre of the mixture and add the egg yolks and almond essence. Using a small spatula or your fingers, gradually work in the dry ingredients. Knead the mixture lightly until it forms a smooth dough. Shape into a ball, wrap in greaseproof paper or foil and chill for 10 minutes.

Sprinkle a board and rolling pin with icing sugar and roll the dough out very thinly. Using a 5-cm (2-inch) pastry cutter, cut the dough into rounds.

Place on greased baking sheets, spaced slightly apart. Put a few almonds on each round. Bake in the centre of the oven for 8–10 minutes or until golden brown. Cool on a wire rack.

# VANILLA KIPFERL

Makes about 48

*225 g (8 oz) butter*
*225 g (8 oz) plain flour, sifted*
*pinch of salt*
*1 tsp vanilla essence*
*100 g (4 oz) ground almonds or hazelnuts or a mixture of both*
*100 g (4 oz) caster sugar*
*sifted icing sugar or caster sugar for coating*

Work the butter into the flour, salt, vanilla essence, nuts and caster sugar until a dough is formed. Chill for 1 hour.

Heat the oven to 160°C (325°F) mark 3. Pinch off pieces of dough the size of a walnut and roll into 'pencils' about 2 cm (¾ inch) thick and 6 cm (2½ inches) long, then bend into crescent shapes. When forming the biscuits, try not to use any flour as this will toughen them; they may be rolled on non-stick parchment.

Arrange the crescents on ungreased baking sheets, leaving about 2.5 cm (1 inch) between each biscuit, to allow them room to spread. Bake for 20 minutes or until a pale golden colour. Leave for 3 minutes to firm up and then remove them from the baking sheets and dip in a bowl of icing or caster sugar.

# ALMOND BISCUITS

Makes about 18

*225 g (8 oz) soft margarine*
*100 g (4 oz) caster sugar*
*50 g (2 oz) ground almonds*
*150 g (6 oz) self-raising flour, sifted*
*a few drops almond essence*
*50 g (2 oz) sultanas*
*40–50 g (1½–2 oz) flaked almonds*

Glaze
*3 tbsp apricot jam*
*1 tbsp water*

Grease an oblong tin about 28 x 18 x 4 cm (11 x 7 x 1½ inches) Heat the oven to 160°C (325°F) mark 3. Cream the fat and sugar together until light and fluffy. Work in the almonds, flour, a few drops of almond essence and the sultanas.

Put into the tin and spread out evenly, making sure the corners are well filled. Sprinkle with the flaked almonds and press in gently. Bake for 50–60 minutes or until lightly browned and just firm.

Heat the apricot jam and water together in a saucepan until melted, then boil for 1 minute. Rub through a sieve and brush over the almonds whilst still warm. Leave in the tin until cold then cut into squares.

# MA' MOULE

*75 g (3 oz) semolina*
*25 g (1 oz) plain flour*
*75 g (3 oz) butter*
*2 tsp boiling water*
*40 g (1½ oz) shelled walnuts, finely chopped*
*40 g (1½ oz) caster sugar*
*½ tsp rose flower water*
*½ tsp orange flower water*
*caster sugar for sprinkling*

Make a dough from the semolina, flour, butter, and boiling water by kneading together. Knead lightly, cover and leave overnight.

The next day, heat the oven to 190°C (375°F) mark 5. Roll the dough into small balls. Make a small hollow in the centre of each one with your fingertip. Blend the walnuts, sugar, rose and orange flower water and use to fill the hollows. Pinch the edges together to cover the filling and then flatten the biscuits with the palm of your hand. Place on greased baking sheets and bake for 10–15 minutes until they are golden brown. While they are still hot, sprinkle them with fine sugar. Cool on a wire rack.

# PETITS FOURS

*1 egg*
*50 g (2 oz) ground almonds*
*50 g (2 oz) caster sugar*
*rice paper*
*angelica to decorate*
*glacé cherries to decorate*

Beat the egg, then mix it to a paste with the almonds and sugar. Place the mixture in a forcing bag fitted with a large star nozzle and pipe small shapes on to baking sheets lined with rice paper. Allow to stand for 24 hours.

Heat the oven to 180°C (350°F) mark 4. Decorate the biscuits with pieces of angelica and halved or quartered cherries and bake for 15–20 minutes or until light brown. Cool on the trays and, when cold, tear apart, removing excess rice paper.

There are many variations on this recipe, and the biscuits can be decorated in many different ways.

# STRAWBERRY DELIGHTS

*5 tbsp butter or margarine*
*225 g (8 oz) dates*
*2 eggs*
*pinch of salt*
*1 tsp vanilla essence*
*100 g (4 oz) rice crispies*
*75 g (3 oz) chopped nuts*
*75 g (3 oz) desiccated coconut*
*100 g (4 oz) granulated sugar*
*a few drops of red food colouring*
*angelica or green marzipan*

Melt the butter in a pan, add the chopped dates and cook over a low heat. When the mixture begins to thicken, add the beaten eggs, salt and vanilla. Allow the mixture to cool a little, then add the rice crispies, nuts and coconut. Turn the mixture on to a large plate and leave to cool.

Make the sugar red by tinting it with the red food colouring. Take small pieces of the mixture and shape them into 'strawberries'. Roll in red sugar. Top each one with a leaf of green angelica or marzipan.

This recipe is excellent for freezing.

# BUTTER KNOTS

Makes about 16

*100 g (4 oz) butter*
*50 g (2 oz) caster sugar*
*1 egg, lightly beaten*
*50 g (2 oz) ground almonds*
*150 g (6 oz) plain flour, sifted*
*flaked almonds*
*50 g (2 oz) icing sugar, sifted*
*a little lemon juice or water to mix*

Grease several baking sheets which will fit into the refrigerator.

Cream the butter and sugar together until light and fluffy then beat in about three-quarters of the egg. Add the ground almonds and flour and work together to form a dough.

Take about half of the mixture, break off small pieces, roll into strips with the hands and then form into fancy knot shapes on the baking sheets. Chill in the refrigerator for at least 30 minutes. Heat the oven to 220°C (425°F) mark 7.

Meanwhile shape the rest of the dough in the same way then brush with the remainder of the egg and sprinkle with the nuts. Chill.

Bake both varieties of knots for 10–15 minutes. Make up the glacé icing and use to brush over the plain knots as soon as they come out of the oven. Remove all to a wire rack and leave to cool and set.

# ALMOND COCOROONS

Makes about 24

*2 egg whites*
*75 g (3 oz) desiccated coconut*
*40 g (1½ oz) ground almonds*
*100 g (4 oz) caster sugar*
*rice paper*

Heat the oven to 160°C (325°F) mark 3. Whisk the egg whites until stiff. Mix the coconut, ground almonds and sugar together and fold lightly into the beaten egg whites.

Place the mixture in small rounds (about 2 teaspoons at a time) on baking sheets lined with rice paper. Bake for 20–25 minutes then cool on a wire rack and pull apart, removing surplus rice paper when cold.

# ALMOND JUMBLES

Makes 16–20

*100 g (4 oz) butter or margarine*
*100 g (4 oz) caster sugar*
*1 egg, beaten*
*almond essence*
*150 g (6 oz) plain flour, sifted*
*50 g (2 oz) ground almonds*

Grease two baking sheets. Heat the oven to 180°C (350°F) mark 4. Cream the fat and sugar together until light and fluffy. Beat in the egg and a few drops of almond essence. Gradually work in the flour and the ground almonds to give a firm but pliable dough, and knead lightly.

Divide the dough into two pieces and roll each into a long sausage 1–2 cm (½–¾ inch) in diameter. Cut into 10-cm (4-inch) lengths and put on to the baking sheets in 'S' shapes. Bake for 15–20 minutes or until a pale golden brown. Cool on a wire rack.

# ALMOND BALLS

Makes about 24

*100 g (4 oz) butter or margarine*
*100 g (4 oz) caster sugar*
*100 g (4 oz) ground almonds*
*1 egg, separated*
*1 tsp vanilla essence*
*100 g (4 oz) plain flour, sifted*
*slivers of almonds*

Heat the oven to 180°C (350°F) mark 4. Cream the butter and sugar together until light and fluffy. Stir in the ground almonds, the egg yolk, vanilla essence and the flour. Knead the dough until it is well blended.

Roll into small balls about 2.5 cm (1 inch) in diameter. Place on a lightly greased baking sheet and press a slivered almond on top of each one. Brush with the slightly beaten egg white and bake for 20–30 minutes. Cool on a wire rack. When cold, store in an airtight container.

# HAZELNUT CRUNCHIES

Makes about 12 pairs

*100 g (4 oz) hazelnuts, toasted*
*100 g (4 oz) butter*
*65 g (2½ oz) caster sugar*
*125 g (5 oz) plain flour*
*2 tbsp thick honey*
*100 g (4 oz) icing sugar, sifted*
*2 tsp coffee essence*
*1 tbsp water*

Grease two or three baking sheets. Heat the oven to 180°C (350°F) mark 4.

Reserve 36 nuts and grind the remainder finely in a mouli grater or blender. Cream the butter and sugar together until light and fluffy. Gradually work in the ground nuts and flour. Cover and chill for about 15 minutes.

Roll the dough out on a floured board to about 3 mm (⅛ inch) thick and cut into 7-cm (2½-inch) rounds using a plain cutter. Lift carefully on to the baking sheets and cook in the centre of the oven for about 10–15 minutes or until lightly coloured. Cool on a wire rack.

For the icing: mix the icing sugar with the coffee essence and sufficient water to give a thick coating consistency. Sandwich the biscuits in pairs with the honey then put a dab of icing on top of each one. Add 3 hazelnuts to each dab of icing and leave to set.

# ORANGE CARAMEL ROLLS

Makes about 16

*75 g (3 oz) butter*
*100 g (4 oz) caster sugar*
*50 g (2 oz) plain flour*
*25 g (1 oz) cornflour*
*grated rind and juice of 1 orange*
*100 g (4 oz) flaked almonds*

Line baking sheets with non-stick parchment. Greese the handles of several wooden spoons. Heat the oven to 180°C (350°F) mark 4. Cream the butter and sugar until light and fluffy. Sift the flour and cornflour together and add to the creamed mixture alternating with the orange rind and juice. Mix in the flaked almonds.

Drop teaspoons of the mixture on to the prepared baking sheets keeping well apart. Bake for about 25 minutes.

Cool on the baking sheets for a few minutes then remove carefully and wind round the wooden spoon handles. Cool on wire racks until firm then slip off and leave on the racks until cold. Store in an airtight container.

# MACAROONIES

Makes about 18

*75 g (3 oz) plain flour*
*25 g (1 oz) ground rice*
*25 g (1 oz) caster sugar*
*50 g (2 oz) butter*
*1 egg yolk*

Topping
*1 egg white*
*75 g (3 oz) caster sugar*
*50 g (2 oz) ground almonds*
*a few drops almond essence*

*a little apricot jam*

Grease two or three baking sheets. Heat the oven to 180°C (350°F) mark 4. Put the flour, rice and sugar in a bowl. Gradually work in the softened butter and the egg yolk and knead lightly together. Roll out on a lightly floured board to about 3 mm (⅛ inch) thick. With a fluted 5-cm (2-inch) cutter, stamp out as many rounds as possible.

Place on the baking sheets. For the topping: whisk the egg white until stiff; fold in the sugar, almonds and almond essence. Place the mixture in a piping bag fitted with a small plain nozzle and pipe a ring around the edge of each biscuit.

Bake for 15–20 minutes until a light brown. Cool on a wire rack and store in an airtight container. Before serving, fill the centre of each biscuit with apricot jam.

# TRADITIONAL AND FOREIGN BISCUITS

This chapter contains a range of well known favourites such as florentines, tuiles, Easter biscuits and Garibaldis, mixed with a selection of foreign biscuits which include Viennese, Belgian, Finnish and German varieties.

# MACAROONS

*2 egg whites*
*100 g (4 oz) ground almonds*
*25 g (1 oz) ground rice*
*225 g (8 oz) caster sugar*
*rice paper*
*a few split almonds*
*egg white for glazing*

Heat the oven to 180°C (350°F) mark 4. Whisk the egg whites until stiff, then fold in the ground almonds, ground rice and sugar.

Line baking sheets with rice paper. Place small heaps of the mixture on the rice paper, spaced out so that there is room for them to spread. Top each one with a split almond and glaze with egg white. Bake for 25–30 minutes. Cool on the baking sheets then break up, tearing off excess rice paper.

# CORNISH GINGER FAIRINGS

*100 g (4 oz) butter*
*100 g (4 oz) caster sugar*
*1 tbsp golden syrup*
*175 g (6 oz) self-raising flour*
*1 tsp ground ginger*
*pinch of bicarbonate of soda*

Heat the oven to 200°C (400°F) mark 6. Melt the butter, sugar and syrup in a pan. Sift the dry ingredients into a bowl and add the melted mixture, stirring to form a dough. Roll the dough into small balls and place on greased baking sheets. Bake for 10–15 minutes or until golden brown. Cool on a wire rack.

# APPLEBY FAIRINGS

*450 g (1 lb) plain flour*
*275 g (10 oz) butter*
*225 g (8 oz) caster sugar*
*pinch of salt*
*1 egg yolk*

Heat the oven to 180–190°C (350–375°F) mark 4–5. Sift the flour into a bowl and rub in the butter until the mixture resembles fine breadcrumbs, then add the sugar and salt. Drop in the egg yolk and work the mixture into a dry dough.

Roll out on a lightly floured board to a thickness of 5 mm (¼ inch) and cut into small rounds. Place on greased baking sheets and impress the biscuits with a pattern or prick them all over. Bake for about 35–40 minutes. Cool on a wire rack.

# KOURABIÉDES

Makes about 40

*225 g (8 oz) butter*
*75 g (3 oz) caster sugar*
*2 tbsp ouzo*
*¼ tsp vanilla essence*
*1 egg yolk*
*275 g (10 oz) plain flour*
*½ tsp baking powder*
*40 whole cloves*
*icing sugar for sprinkling*
*rose water*

Heat the oven to 190°C (375°F) mark 5. Cream the butter and sugar until light and fluffy. Beat in the ouzo, vanilla essence and egg yolk. Sift the flour and baking powder and add to the mixture. Mix well to make a firm dough.

Roll rounded teaspoons of the dough into balls and place on baking sheets lined with non-stick baking parchment. Flatten slightly and spike each cookie with a clove. Bake for 20 minutes.

Transfer the cookies immediately to a wire rack and, while they are still hot, sprinkle with icing sugar and rose water. Leave until cold.

# FLORENTINES

*150 ml (¼ pint) single cream*
*75 g (3 oz) caster sugar*
*75 g (3 oz) glacé cherries, mixed peel and raisins, mixed*
*100 g (4 oz) flaked almonds*
*2 tsp butter*
*1 scant tbsp self-raising flour*

Topping
*175 g (6 oz) block plain chocolate*

Heat the oven to 190°C (375°F) mark 5. Heat the cream and sugar slowly in a thick saucepan until the sugar has dissolved. Bring to the boil, then tip in the chopped fruit, nuts, butter and flour. Remove from the heat and mix thoroughly with a wooden spoon.

Line a baking sheet with non-stick baking parchment. Place small teaspoons of the mixture 15 cm (6 inches) apart on the baking sheet. Bake for about 10 minutes, or until evenly browned. Remove the biscuits at once from the sheet and cool them on a wire rack.

For the topping: melt the chocolate in a basin over hot water. When the biscuits are cold, spread their undersides with melted chocolate and mark the chocolate with a fork. Leave the biscuits upside down on a flat surface to dry.

# GARIBALDI BISCUITS

*200 g (7 oz) self-raising flour*
*25 g (1 oz) cornflour*
*50 g (2 oz) caster sugar*
*pinch of salt*
*50 g (2 oz) butter or margarine*
*1 egg yolk*
*a little milk*
*75–100 g (3–4 oz) currants*
*caster sugar for sprinkling*

Heat the oven to 200°C (400°F) mark 6. Sift the flour, cornflour, sugar and salt into a bowl. Rub in the butter until the mixture resembles breadcrumbs. Mix to a stiffish dough with the egg yolk and milk.

Turn on to a floured board and roll the dough out to a thin oblong. Trim the edges then sprinkle one half of the dough with the currants. Fold over the other half of the dough and press the edges well together.

Roll the dough out lightly with a floured rolling pin until it is about 2.5 mm (⅛ inch) thick. Cut into 5-cm (2-inch) squares. Place on greased baking sheets and bake for 15 minutes or until golden brown. Sprinkle with caster sugar and cool on a wire rack.

# LANCASHIRE NUTS

*100 g (4 oz) butter*
*100 g (4 oz) caster sugar*
*1 egg*
*100 g (4 oz) plain flour*
*100 g (4 oz) cornflour*
*1 tbsp baking powder*

Filling
*50 g (2 oz) butter*
*100 g (4 oz) icing sugar*
*a few drops of vanilla essence*

Heat the oven to 180°C (350°F) mark 4. For the biscuits: cream the butter and sugar until light and fluffy. Add the egg and beat together. Sift together the flour, cornflour and baking powder, add to the mixture and work to form a paste. Place teaspoons of the dough on a greased baking sheet and bake for 8–10 minutes until golden brown.

To make the filling: cream the butter until it is soft. Gradually add the sifted icing sugar and cream together. Add the vanilla essence and beat the mixture well.

When they are cold, sandwich the biscuits together in pairs with the filling.

# DANISH SPECIER BISCUITS

Makes 40

*225 g (8 oz) plain flour*
*75 g (3 oz) icing sugar*
*175 g (6 oz) butter or margarine*
*25 g (1 oz) blanched almonds, chopped*
*granulated sugar to coat*

Sift the flour and icing sugar into a bowl and rub in the fat. Stir in the almonds and mix to form a dough. Shape the dough into two 'sausages' about 5 cm (2 inches) thick and roll in granulated sugar until they are completely covered. Wrap in cling film or foil and chill until firm.

Heat the oven to 200°C (400°F) mark 6. Cut the dough into 5-mm (¼-inch) thick slices and place on ungreased baking sheets. Bake for 8–10 minutes until light brown around the edges. Cool on a wire rack.

# GRASMERE GINGERBREAD

Makes about 18

*450 g (1 lb) plain flour*
*2 tsp ground ginger*
*1 tsp bicarbonate of soda*
*1 tsp cream of tartar*
*225 g (8 oz) soft brown sugar*
*225 g (8 oz) butter or margarine*

Heat the oven to 150°C (300°F) mark 2. Sift the flour, ginger, soda and cream of tartar into a bowl, stir in the sugar and then rub in the fat until the mixture resembles fine breadcrumbs. Press the mixture into a greased tin 25 x 30 cm (10 x 12 inches) lined with greased greaseproof paper. Bake for about 30 minutes. Allow the gingerbread to cool slightly before cutting into pieces. Remove from the tin when cold.

# GRANTHAM GINGER DROPS

Makes about 24

*100 g (4 oz) butter or margarine*
*100 g (4 oz) caster sugar*
*100 g (4 oz) self-raising flour*
*2 tsp ground ginger*

Heat the oven to 125°C (250°F) mark ½. Lightly cream the fat and sugar together until soft, but do not cream too much. Sift the flour and ginger together and work into the mixture to form a stiff dough.

Roll the dough into small balls and place on ungreased baking sheets. Bake for 30–40 minutes. Cool on a wire rack.

# EASTER BISCUITS

*75 g (3 oz) butter*
*75 g (3 oz) caster sugar*
*1 egg yolk*
*pinch of mixed spice*
*50 g (2 oz) currants*
*15 g (½ oz) mixed peel*
*175 g (6 oz) plain flour, sifted*
*a little milk*

Glaze
*1 egg white*
*caster sugar*

Heat the oven to 180°C (350°F) mark 4. Soften the butter, add the sugar, and cream the mixture until light and fluffy. Add the egg yolk, spice, peel and flour and mix to a stiff dough with the milk. Roll the dough out thinly on a floured board and cut into rounds about 7.5 cm (3 inches) in diameter, using a plain or fluted cutter. Place on greased baking sheets and bake for 15–20 minutes. After 10 minutes, brush with the egg white and sprinkle with caster sugar, then return to the oven until a light golden brown. Cool on a wire rack.

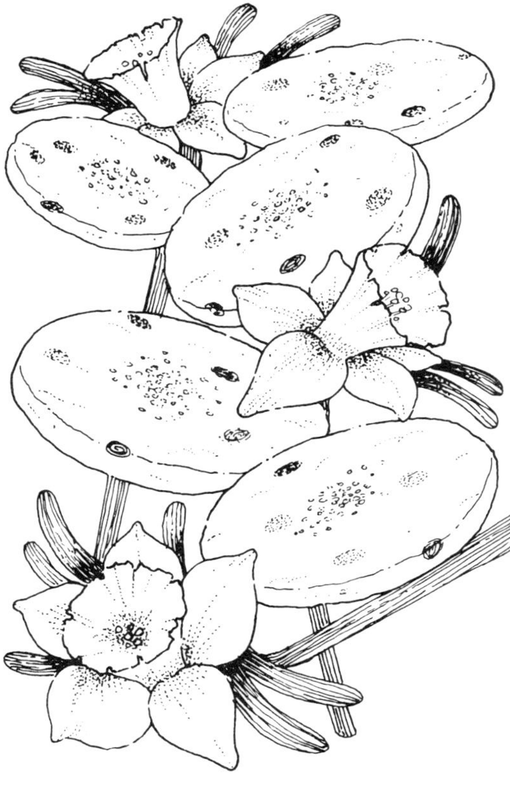

# BELGIAN SUGAR BISCUITS

*75 g (3 oz) butter*
*150 g (5 oz) caster sugar*
*1 egg yolk*
*175 g (6 oz) plain flour*
*1 tsp ground ginger*

Cream the butter and sugar until light and fluffy, then add the egg yolk. Add the sifted flour and ginger, and mix thoroughly. Shape the dough into a 5-cm (2-inch) diameter roll, wrap and leave in the refrigerator until firm.

Heat the oven to 160°C (325°F) mark 3. Using a sharp knife, cut the roll into thin slices approximately 5 mm (¼ inch) thick. Place on greased baking sheets and bake for about 15–20 minutes until the biscuits are lightly browned. Cool on a wire rack.

# VIENNESE BISCUITS

*100 g (4 oz) butter or margarine*
*25 g (1 oz) icing sugar*
*a few drops of vanilla essence*
*100 g (4 oz) plain flour, sifted*
*glacé cherries*

Heat the oven to 180°C (350°F) mark 4. Cream the butter and sugar until light and fluffy, stir in the essence and gradually work in the flour.

Put the mixture in a forcing bag fitted with a large star nozzle and pipe fingers, rounds, or other shapes on to greased baking sheets. Decorate each with a cherry or piece of cherry. Bake for 15–20 minutes. Leave to cool before removing from the baking sheet. Store in an airtight container.

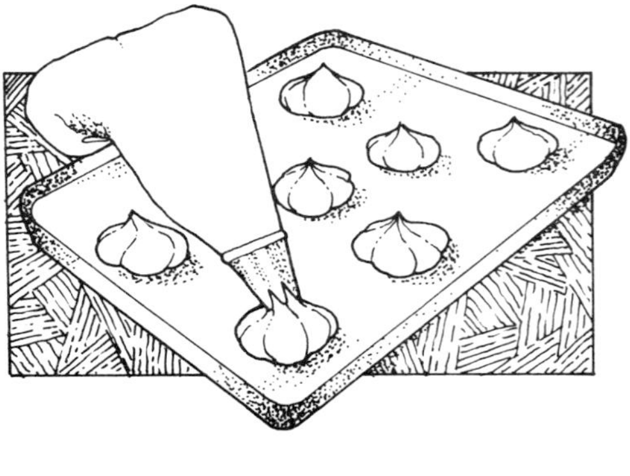

# FINNISH SHORTBREAD

*350 g (12 oz) plain flour*
*225 g (8 oz) butter*
*100 g (4 oz) caster sugar*
*1 egg yolk*

Coating
*2–3 egg yolks*
*chopped almonds*
*granulated sugar*

Heat the oven to 180°C (350°F) mark 4. Sift the flour into a bowl and rub in the butter until the mixture resembles fine breadcrumbs. Add the egg yolk and work to form a dough and knead lightly. Roll the dough into long 'sausages' the thickness of your little finger and cut into 1-cm (½-inch) lengths.

Dip the pieces of dough in the beaten egg yolks, then roll in a mixture of chopped almonds and sugar. Place on greased baking sheets and bake for 20 minutes until golden brown. Cool on a wire rack.

# JUMBLES

*225 g (8 oz) plain flour*
*175 g (6 oz) butter*
*225 g (8 oz) caster sugar*
*finely grated rind of 1 lemon*
*1 egg (size 1 or 2), beaten*
*caster sugar for dredging*

Heat the oven to 180°C (350°F) mark 4. Sift the flour into a bowl and rub in the butter until the mixture resembles breadcrumbs. Add the sugar and the lemon rind and then stir in the beaten egg and work to form into a smooth dough.

Roll the dough into long thin 'sausages'. Cut them into 10-cm (4-inch) lengths and make them into wheel or 'S' shapes. Place on greased baking sheets and bake for 15–20 minutes or until evenly browned. Dredge with caster sugar immediately and cool on a wire rack.

# BRANDY CORNETS

Makes 12–16

*50 g (2 oz) butter or blended white vegetable fat*
*50 g (2 oz) golden syrup*
*50 g (2 oz) caster sugar*
*50 g (2 oz) plain flour*
*a large pinch of ground ginger*

Line two baking sheets with non-stick parchment. Grease the outer surface of several cream horn tins. Heat the oven to 160°C (325°F) mark 3.

Melt the fat in a saucepan with the syrup and sugar, then remove from the heat. Sift the flour with the ginger and stir into the melted mixture.

Put teaspoons of the mixture well apart on the baking sheets and cook for 8–10 minutes or until golden brown. Cool until just firm enough to remove with a palette knife then wind quickly round the cream horn tins. Cool on a wire rack until firm then slip off the tins. Repeat with the remaining mixture. Serve as they are or fill with whipped cream.

# BOURBON BISCUITS

*100 g (4 oz) plain flour*
*15 g (½ oz) cocoa*
*½ tsp baking powder*
*50 g (2 oz) butter*
*50 g (2 oz) caster sugar*
*1 tbsp golden syrup*
*granulated sugar to coat*

Filling
*25 g (1 oz) plain chocolate*
*1½ tbsp water*
*50 g (2 oz) icing sugar, sifted*
*a few drops of vanilla essence*

Heat the oven to 160°C (325°F) mark 3. To make the biscuits: sift together the flour, cocoa and baking powder. Cream the butter and caster sugar until light and fluffy then beat in the syrup and stir in half the flour mixture. Turn the dough on to a lightly floured board and knead in the remaining flour mixture. Roll the dough out to a thickness of 5 mm (¼ inch), sprinkle with granulated sugar and press the sugar in with a rolling pin. Cut into neat fingers and place on a greased baking sheet. Bake for 15–20 minutes. Cool on a wire rack.

For the filling: melt the chocolate in the water, add the icing sugar and essence, and beat together until smooth. When the biscuits are cool, sandwich together with the filling.

# GERMAN BISCUITS

*200 g (7 oz) plain flour*
*½ tsp baking powder*
*½ tsp ground cinnamon*
*100 g (4 oz) butter or margarine*
*100 g (4 oz) caster sugar*
*1 egg, beaten*

Filling
*raspberry jam*

Icing
*150 g (6 oz) icing sugar*
*1½ tbsp water*

*glacé cherries to decorate*

Heat the oven to 180°C (350°F) mark 4. For the biscuits: sift the flour, baking powder and cinnamon into a bowl, then rub in the fat until the mixture resembles fine breadcrumbs. Add the sugar and mix to a stiff dough with the egg.

Roll the dough out to a thickness of 2.5 mm (⅛ inch) and cut into rounds about 5 cm (2 inches) in diameter. Place on greased baking sheets and bake for 10–15 minutes.

When the biscuits are cold, sandwich together with the jam. To make the icing: mix the sifted icing sugar with the water and beat until smooth. Ice the tops of the biscuits, then decorate with halved or quartered glacé cherries.

These biscuits taste even better if made the day before they are eaten.

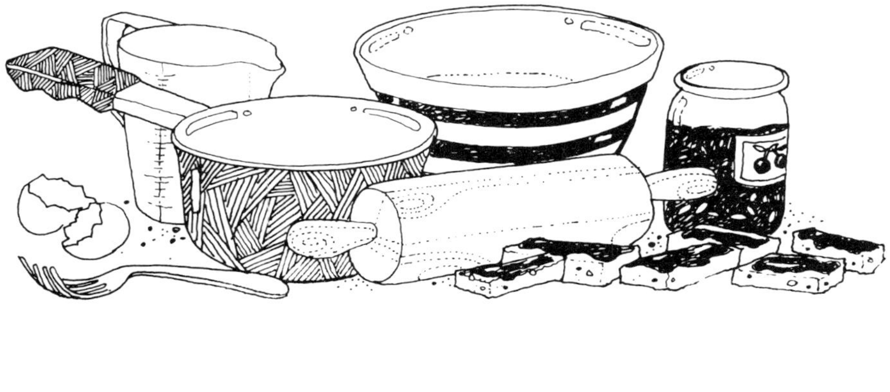

## SHREWSBURY BISCUITS

*100 g (4 oz) butter*
*100 g (4 oz) caster sugar*
*1 egg*
*grated rind and juice of ½ lemon*
*25 g (1 oz) currants*
*225 g (8 oz) plain flour*
*pinch of bicarbonate of soda*

Cream the butter and sugar until light and fluffy, then beat in the egg, lemon rind and juice and the currants. Sift the flour and soda and work into the mixture. Knead well, cover and leave in the refrigerator overnight. Heat the oven to 180°C (350°F) mark 4. Roll the dough out to a thickness of 5 mm (¼ inch) and cut into rounds approx 6 cm (2½ inches) in diameter. Place on greased baking sheets and bake for about 20 minutes. Cool on a wire rack.

## SHORTBREAD BISCUITS

*150 g (6 oz) plain flour*
*100 g (4 oz) butter*
*50 g (2 oz) caster sugar*
*caster sugar for dredging*

Sift the flour into a bowl, add the other ingredients and knead until the mixture has a soft consistency. Roll out on a floured board and cut into fingers. Place on lightly greased baking sheets and leave overnight. Heat the oven to 200°C (400°F) mark 6. Bake for 10–12 minutes or until golden brown. Dredge with caster sugar and cool on a wire rack.

## GERMAN ALMOND BISCUITS

*225 g (8 oz) butter*
*175 g (6 oz) caster sugar*
*1 egg*
*100 g (4 oz) self-raising flour*
*100 g (4 oz) plain flour*
*raspberry jam*
*1 tsp sugar for glazing*
*flaked almonds*

Heat the oven to 150°C (300°F) mark 2. Cream the butter and sugar until light and fluffy and then add the beaten egg (keeping back a small quantity for glazing). Sift in the flours and mix well.

Divide the mixture in half and use one portion to cover the base of a well greased cake tin 18 cm (7 inches) in diameter. Spread this with raspberry jam then cover the jam with the remaining mixture.

Add a teaspoon of sugar to the remainder of the egg and use to glaze the dough, then sprinkle with flaked almonds. Bake for 45 minutes. Leave in the tin until almost cold, then cut into slices. Remove from the tin when quite cold.

This is equally good if the jam is omitted, but the mixture should then be spread over a larger tin.

# TUILES

*50 g (2 oz) butter*
*50 g (2 oz) caster sugar*
*2 egg whites*
*50 g (2 oz) plain flour*
*pinch of salt*
*grated rind of ½ lemon or a few drops of vanilla essence*

Heat the oven to 190°C (375°F) mark 5. Soften the butter in a bowl over hot water but do not let it get oily. Beat lightly with a fork, gradually adding the sugar, until very light and fluffy. Beat in the unwhisked egg whites a little at a time.

Sift the flour with the salt into a bowl and fold into the mixture gently. Flavour with lemon rind or vanilla essence. Put into a forcing bag fitted with a 1-cm (½-inch) nozzle and pipe 5-cm (2-inch) lengths on to baking sheets lined with non-stick parchment, allowing room for the biscuits to spread. Bake for 10 minutes until golden brown around the edges.

While the Tuiles are still warm, remove from the baking sheets carefully and lay over a greased rolling pin to make them curl. Leave until cold.

These biscuits are usually served with a rich party dessert, special poached fruit or fresh soft drinks.

# KICHELECH

*225 g (8 oz) hard margarine or 100 g (4 oz) butter and 100 g (4 oz) margarine*
*450 g (1 lb) self-raising flour*
*175 g (6 oz) caster sugar*
*2 tsp ground almonds*
*1 egg*
*milk or white wine to make a pliable dough*

Heat the oven to 180°C (350°F) mark 4. Rub the margarine into the flour using fingertips. Add the sugar and ground almonds and mix to a pliable dough with the beaten egg and milk or white wine. Roll out thinly and then cut into rounds using a plain cutter. Moisten and sprinkle with sugar. Place on greased trays and cook until light brown – about 15 minutes.

# QUICK KICHELECH

Makes 36

*2 large eggs*
*150 ml (¼ pint) cooking oil*
*2 tsp vanilla essence*
*1 tsp grated lemon rind*
*150–175 g (5–6 oz) caster sugar*
*225 g (8 oz) self raising flour*
*sugar and chopped nuts for decoration*

Heat the oven to 200°C (400°F) mark 6. Beat the eggs until well blended. Stir in the oil, vanilla and lemon rind. Beat in the sugar until the mixture thickens, then stir in the flour, making a soft, thick batter.

Drop the batter from a teaspoon on to a greased baking tin, leaving 5 cm (2 inch) between the biscuits. Dip the bottom of a tumbler in oil and then in granulated sugar and use to flatten each biscuit gently.

Sprinkle with chopped nuts or dessicated coconut. Cook for 10 minutes or until golden brown.

This Jewish recipe makes a very economical batch of biscuits.

# PASSOVER MERINGUES

*2 egg whites*
*175 g (6 oz) caster or icing sugar*
*100 g (4 oz) raisins*
*50 g (2 oz) chopped nuts*

Heat the oven to 150°C (300°F) mark 2.

Beat the egg whites until stiff. Add the sugar a spoonful at a time and beat until stiff after each addition. Carefully fold in the raisins and nuts. Place in small heaps on a greased baking tray or a baking tray lined with non-stick parchment. Cook for about 30 minutes, until crisp.

For the week of Passover, the Jewish festival celebrating the Exodus from Egypt, no flour is eaten. This recipe is one of the many delicious ways round the problem of baking without flour.

# DUTCH JANHAGEL

*100 g (4 oz) unsalted butter*
*150 g (6 oz) plain flour*
*75 g (3 oz) caster sugar*
*½ tsp ground cinnamon*
*25 g (1 oz) flaked almonds*
*a little granulated sugar*

Grease a Swiss roll tin measuring about 25 x 18 cm (10 x 6 inches). Heat the oven to 180°C (350°F) mark 4.

Rub the butter into the sifted flour then add the caster sugar and cinnamon and work together to form a dough.

Roll out to form a rectangle, then press into the prepared tin and smooth with a round-bladed knife. Sprinkle with chopped almonds and a little granulated sugar and bake just above the centre of the oven for 20–25 minutes, until golden brown.

Cut into fingers while still warm then leave until firm and remove carefully to a wire rack and leave until cold. Store in an airtight container.

# SAVOURY BISCUITS

No book of biscuits would be complete without a section on savoury biscuits. These are all crisp and tasty to serve plain, with cheese or with a savoury topping. They are also ideal for cocktail nibbles to use with dips, or as canapé bases.

# BACON AND OATMEAL BISCUITS

Makes about 30

*100 g (4 oz) hard margarine*
*100 g (4 oz) rolled oats*
*100 g (4 oz) self-raising flour*
*salt and pepper*
*1 tsp dry mustard*
*75–100 g (3–4 oz) lean bacon, finely minced*
*1 small egg*

Heat the oven to 180°C (350°F) mark 4. Rub the margarine into the oats and sifted flour until the mixture resembles breadcrumbs. Add the salt and pepper, mustard and bacon. Mix thoroughly then add sufficient beaten egg to mix to a dough.

Roll the dough out fairly thinly on a floured board and cut into any shape required. Place on greased baking sheets and bake for 15 minutes or until golden brown. Cool on a wire rack.

# CRACKAMACS

*100 g (4 oz) self-raising flour*
*½ tsp salt*
*milk or water to mix*

Heat the oven to 200°C (400°F) mark 6. Sift the flour and salt into a basin. Add the milk or water and mix with a fork to make a dough.

Roll the dough out very thinly on a floured board and cut into rounds or squares. Place on greased baking sheets and bake for 10–15 minutes. Cool on a wire rack. Serve with cheese.

# OATCAKES

*225 g (8 oz) plain flour*
*1 tsp salt*
*1 tsp bicarbonate of soda*
*1 tbsp caster sugar*
*450 g (1 lb) medium oatmeal*
*100 g (4 oz) margarine, melted*
*5 tbsp lukewarm water*

Heat the oven to 190°C (375°F) mark 5. Sift the flour, salt and soda into a bowl. Mix in the sugar and oatmeal and bind together with the melted margarine and water.

Roll the dough out on a floured board to a thickness of about 2.5 mm (⅛ inch) and cut into 5-cm (2-inch) rounds. Place on greased baking sheets and bake for 20 minutes. Cool on a wire rack. These taste very good when served with cheese.

# GUERNSEY BISCUITS

Makes about 40

*25 g (1 oz) fresh yeast or 15 g (½ oz) dried yeast*
*15 g (½ oz) caster sugar*
*250 ml (8 fl oz) warm milk or water*
*450 g (1 lb) plain flour*
*15 g (½ oz) salt*
*100 g (4 oz) margarine*

Heat the oven to 200°C (400°F) mark 6. Cream together the yeast and sugar and add the liquid (or sprinkle the dried yeast and sugar on the liquid). Leave in a warm place until frothy. Sift the flour and salt into a bowl and rub in the fat until the mixture resembles fine breadcrumbs. Add the yeast mixture to the flour and knead well. Cover and leave the dough to rise in a warm place for 1 hour.

Knock back the dough and knead again. Form into balls about 2 cm (1 inch) in diameter. Flatten the balls and roll out thinly. Place on greased baking sheets and allow them to prove for 15–20 minutes in a warm place. Bake for 20 minutes.

# WHOLEMEAL SAVOURY TITBITS

Makes 8–12

*100 g (4 oz) wholemeal flour*
*½ tsp baking powder*
*pinch of salt*
*25 g (1 oz) lard*
*milk to mix*

Topping
*4 tbsp cream cheese*
*1 tbsp grated cheese*
*1 tbsp chopped celery*
*salt, pepper and mustard to taste*
*parsley and red pepper to garnish*

Heat the oven to 180°C (350°F) mark 4. For the biscuits: mix together the flour, baking powder and salt in a bowl. Rub in the lard until the mixture resembles breadcrumbs, then add sufficient milk to make a stiff dough. Roll the dough out very thinly on a floured board. Prick the dough and cut into small rounds approximately 4 cm (1½ inches) in diameter. Place on greased baking sheets and bake for 10–15 minutes until the biscuits are brown and firm. Cool on a wire rack. When they are cold, store in an airtight container.

To make the topping: mix the cream cheese, grated cheese and chopped celery. Season with salt, pepper and a little mustard. Pile this mixture on to the biscuits and garnish with sprigs of parsley and/or strips of red pepper.

# PAPRIKA CHEESE BISCUITS

*175 g (6 oz) plain flour*
*½ tsp paprika*
*175 g (6 oz) butter*
*75 g (3 oz) Cheddar cheese, finely grated*
*1 egg yolk*
*50 g (2 oz) unblanched almonds, chopped*
*beaten egg to glaze*
*extra cheese or paprika to decorate*

Heat the oven to 160°C (325°F) mark 3. Sift the flour and paprika into a bowl and rub in the butter. Add the finely grated cheese and lightly beaten egg yolk. Stir in the nuts and work the mixture to a smooth dough.

Roll the dough out on a floured board to a thickness of 1 cm (½ inch). Cut into shapes with a small plain cutter and place on greased baking sheets. Brush the tops with beaten egg and sprinkle lightly with a little more cheese or paprika. Bake for about 20 minutes. Cool on a wire rack.

# CHEESE STRAWS

*50 g (2 oz) cheese*
*½ tsp salt*
*pinch of pepper*
*pinch of cayenne*
*75 g (3 oz) plain flour, sifted*
*50 g (2 oz) margarine or butter*

Heat the oven to 180°C (350°F) mark 4. Rub the cheese through a wire sieve. Add the salt, pepper and cayenne to the flour. Partly cream the fat, then add the cheese and the seasoned flour. Mix it to a paste and allow to stand for at least 30 minutes, preferably in the refrigerator.

Roll the dough out on a lightly floured board and cut into straws or biscuits. Place on a greased baking sheet and prick well. Cook for about 15 minutes and cool on a wire rack.

# DIGESTIVE BISCUITS

*175 g (6 oz) wholewheat flour*
*25 g (1 oz) oatmeal*
*½ tsp salt*
*1 tsp baking powder*
*75 g (3 oz) butter or margarine*
*40 g (1½ oz) soft brown sugar*
*2–3 tbsp milk*

Heat the oven to 190°C (375°F) mark 5. Mix together the flour and oatmeal. Sift in the salt and baking powder and rub in the fat until the mixture resembles breadcrumbs. Stir in the sugar and add sufficient milk to mix to a stiff dough.

Roll the dough out thinly on a floured board and prick well. Cut 6-cm (2½-inch) rounds with a plain cutter. Place on lightly greased baking sheets and bake for 15–20 minutes. Cool on a wire rack. Serve with cheese.

# CURRY KNOTS

Makes about 18

*100 g (4 oz) plain flour*
*2 tsp curry powder*
*pinch of salt*
*50 g (2 oz) margarine*
*egg yolk or water to mix*
*egg yolk to glaze*

Heat the oven to 180°C (350°F) mark 4. Sift the flour, curry powder and salt into a bowl, and rub in the fat until the mixture resembles fine breadcrumbs. Bind the mixture to a stiff but pliable dough with a little egg yolk or water.

Knead the dough well to remove any cracks and roll it out on a floured board into a long strip about 2 cm (¾ inch) thick. Cut into 15-cm (6-inch) long pieces and tie each one into a knot. Place on a greased baking sheet and brush with beaten egg yolk. Bake for about 10–15 minutes or until golden brown. Cool on a wire rack.

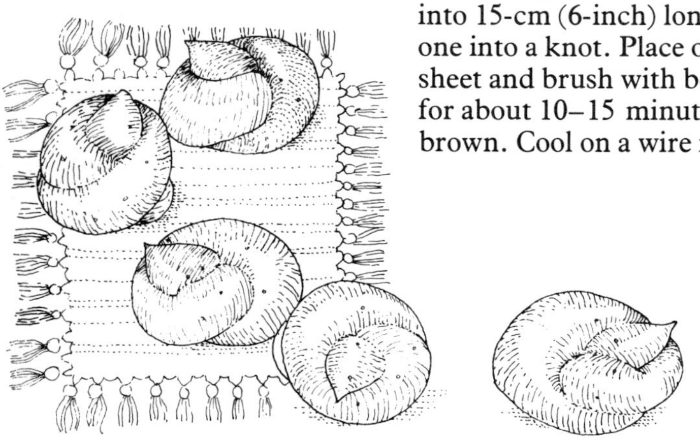

# CHEESE SABLÉS

*75 g (3 oz) plain flour*
*75 g (3 oz) butter*
*75 g (3 oz) cheese, grated*
*salt and pepper to taste*
*1 egg*

Heat the oven to 190°C (375°F) mark 5. Sift the flour into a bowl. Cut the butter into pieces and rub into the flour. Add the grated cheese and season with the salt and pepper. Work the mixture together to make a dough. Wrap the dough in greaseproof paper or foil and chill in the refrigerator for about 30 minutes.

Roll out the dough carefully on a floured board until it is fairly thin. Cut into strips about 5 cm (2 inches) wide and brush with the lightly beaten egg. Cut the strips into triangles and place on a baking sheet lined with greaseproof paper. Bake for 10 minutes until the biscuits are golden brown. Cool on a wire rack.

# WALNUT SAVOURY BISCUITS

*175 g (6 oz) plain flour*
*½ tsp salt*
*½ tsp dry mustard*
*pinch of pepper*
*50 g (2 oz) rolled oats*
*75 g (3 oz) margarine*
*75 g (3 oz) Cheddar cheese, grated*
*50 g (2 oz) walnuts, chopped*
*1 egg*
*150 ml (¼ pint) cold water*
*a few chopped nuts to garnish*

Sift together the flour, salt, mustard and pepper, add the oats and rub in the margarine until the mixture resembles breadcrumbs. Stir in the grated cheese and walnuts. Beat the egg and reserve a teaspoonful for the glaze. Add the remaining egg to the mixture and bind to a stiff dough with sufficient water.

Roll out the mixture on a floured board and trim to make a rectangle. Add a pinch of salt to the remaining egg and brush over the surface. Sprinkle the top with a few chopped nuts. Cut into shapes and place on greased baking sheets. Bake for 12–15 minutes. Cool on a wire rack.

# CHEESE BISCUITS

*225 g (8 oz) plain flour*
*1 tsp baking powder*
*good pinch of salt*
*pinch of cayenne*
*75 g (3 oz) butter*
*225 g (8 oz) cheese, grated*
*1 egg yolk*
*cold water*

Heat the oven to 200°C (400°F) mark 6. Sift the flour, baking powder, salt and cayenne into a bowl. Rub in the butter, until the mixture resembles fine breadcrumbs. Stir in the cheese. Beat the egg yolk with a little cold water, add to the rest of the ingredients and mix to form a stiff dough.

Knead lightly on a floured board, roll out thinly and cut into rounds. Place on greased baking sheets and bake for 10–15 minutes until a pale golden brown. Cool on a wire rack.

# CHEESE CRACKERS

*100 g (4 oz) self-raising flour*
*pinch of salt*
*25 g (1 oz) cheese, finely grated*
*cold water*
*50 g (2 oz) butter or margarine*

Heat the oven to 160°C (325°F) mark 3. Sift the flour and salt into a bowl, then add the finely grated cheese. Mix to a firm dough with the cold water and knead the mixture until it is smooth.

Roll the dough out into an oblong 23 x 12.5 cm (9 x 5 inches) and mark lightly into three portions. Spread 25 g (1 oz) of the butter over the top two-thirds of the dough. Fold the unbuttered portion upwards and top third downwards, envelope fashion. Give the dough a half-turn, and roll it out again, a little larger than the original oblong. Repeat the process with the remainder of the butter, and fold it again. Cover and put in a cool place for 30 minutes.

Roll the dough out and fold it once more (with no fat), then roll it out thinly to less than 5 mm (¼ inch) thick. Cut into squares. Place on lightly greased baking sheets, prick all over and bake for 15–20 minutes. Cool on a wire rack.

# CELERY BISCUITS

*225 g (8 oz) plain flour*
*pinch of salt*
*50 g (2 oz) margarine*
*2 tsp celery seeds*
*top of the milk or single cream*

Heat the oven to 200°C (400°F) mark 6. Sift the flour and salt into a bowl. Rub in the fat until the mixture resembles fine breadcrumbs then add the celery seeds. Add sufficient liquid to mix to a stiff, pliable dough. Knead thoroughly, roll out thinly on a floured board and cut into rounds. Place on greased baking sheets and bake for 10–15 minutes. Cool the biscuits on a wire rack.

Serve alone, with butter or cheese, or with both.

# SAVOURY CURLS

Makes about 40

*50 g (2 oz) margarine*
*1 rounded tsp Marmite*
*100 g (4 oz) plain flour, sieved*
*40 g (1½ oz) cheese, grated*
*water to mix*

Heat the oven to 200°C (400°F) mark 6. Blend the margarine and Marmite together and leave in a cool place for about 15 minutes. Rub the creamed mixture into the flour and add the cheese. Mix to a stiff dough with a little water.

Roll out to a rectangle about 15 cm x 20 cm (6 x 8 inches) and cut into strips about 1 cm (½ inch) wide. Cut each strip into two and twist slightly. Place on greased baking sheets and bake for 5–8 minutes until pale golden brown. Cool on wire racks.

## CREAM CRACKERS

*450 g (1 lb) plain flour*
*1 tsp baking powder*
*pinch of salt*
*100 g (4 oz) butter or lard*
*water or milk to mix*

Heat the oven to 180°C (350°F) mark 4. Sift the flour, salt and baking powder into a bowl. Rub in the butter until the mixture resembles breadcrumbs. Add sufficient water or milk to make a stiff dough.

Roll out very thinly indeed and cut into squares. Place on greased baking sheets and prick well. Bake for about 20 minutes until crisp. Cool on a wire rack.

Serve spread with butter and thinly spread with Marmite, sandwiched together.

## RED CHEESE BISCUITS

*50 g (2 oz) red cheese, grated*
*50 g (2 oz) margarine*
*50 g (2 oz) plain flour*

Heat the oven to 180°C (350°F) mark 4. Rub the margarine and cheese into the flour until a firm paste is formed. No liquid need be added. Roll out very thinly and cut into shapes. Place on a greased baking sheet and bake in the centre of the oven for 5–7 minutes. Cool on a wire rack.

## CHEESE WAFERS

*50 g (2 oz) butter*
*50 g (2 oz) cheese, grated*
*100 g (4 oz) plain flour*
*pinch of salt*
*pinch of dry mustard*
*½ tsp Worcestershire sauce*
*salt for sprinkling*

Heat the oven to 190°C (375°F) mark 5. Cream together the butter and grated cheese. Sieve together the flour and seasonings and work into the creamed mixture with a fork. Add the Worcestershire sauce and knead lightly to form a smooth, firm dough.

Roll out thinly and cut into small squares or rounds. Place on a greased baking sheet and bake for about 8–10 minutes in the centre of the oven. Sprinkle with salt while hot. Cool on a wire rack.

# SAVOURY COCONUT TOASTIES

Makes 24

*50 g (2 oz) plain flour*
*pinch of cayenne pepper*
*pinch of salt*
*pinch of cinnamon*
*100 g (4 oz) Cheddar cheese, grated*
*50 g (2 oz) coconut, toasted*
*1 egg, separated*

Heat the oven to 200°C (400°F) mark 6. Sift the flour, cayenne, salt and cinnamon into a bowl. Add the cheese, coconut and egg yolk and mix all together. Whisk the egg white until stiff and fold into the mixture. Form teaspoonfuls into pyramids and place on well greased baking sheets. Bake for 10 minutes. Cool on wire racks or serve hot.

# CHEESE AND TOMATO BISCUITS

*50 g (2 oz) margarine*
*100 g (4 oz) plain flour, sifted*
*50 g (2 oz) cheese, grated*
*2 tbsp tomato sauce, preferably homemade*
*water to mix*

Filling
*cheese spread or cream cheese*

Heat the oven to 200°C (400°F) mark 6. Rub the margarine into the flour until the mixture resembles fine breadcrumbs. Add the grated cheese and the tomato sauce and mix to a stiff dough.

Roll out and cut into shapes as desired. Place on a greased baking sheet and bake for 10–15 minutes. Cool on a wire rack.

When cold, sandwich together with cheese spread or cream cheese.

FLOU

# WHAT IS THE WI ?

If you have enjoyed this book, the chances are that you would enjoy belonging to the largest women's organisation in the country — the Women's Institutes.

We are friendly, go-ahead, like-minded women, who derive enormous satisfaction from all the movement has to offer. This list is long — you can make new friends, have fun and companionship, visit new places, develop new skills, take part in community services, fight local campaigns, become a WI market producer, and play an active role in an organisation which has a national voice.

The WI is the only women's organisation in the country which owns an adult education establishment. At Denman College, you can take a course in anything from car maintenance to paper sculpture, from book binding to yoga, or cordon bleu cookery to fly-fishing.

All you need to do to join is write to us here at the **National Federation of Women's Institutes, 39 Eccleston Street, London SW1W 9NT**, or telephone 01-730 7212, and we will put you in touch with WIs in your immediate locality. We hope to hear from you.

**Biscuits for shows**

Please note that if you wish to enter homemade biscuits in a show, it is important to check the schedule first with regard to the quantity and variety. Biscuits, by definition, should be crisp; they should be even in size and colour, of a good shape and not too thick.

Some of the recipes in this book may not be accepted by judges for shows because they may not all fall within the definitions of the schedule.

# INDEX